THE FRENCH LITTELTON
1609

T0382274

The French Littelton

By CLAUDIUS HOLYBAND

The Edition of 1609

WITH AN INTRODUCTION BY
M. ST CLARE BYRNE

CAMBRIDGE
At the University Press
1953

CAMBRIDGE
UNIVERSITY PRESS

University Printing House, Cambridge CB2 8BS, United Kingdom

Cambridge University Press is part of the University of Cambridge.

It furthers the University's mission by disseminating knowledge in the pursuit of
education, learning and research at the highest international levels of excellence.

www.cambridge.org
Information on this title: www.cambridge.org/9781107480292

© Cambridge University Press 1953

First published 1953
First paperback edition 2014

A catalogue record for this publication is available from the British Library

ISBN 978-1-107-48029-2 Paperback

CONTENTS

INTRODUCTION

CLAUDIUS HOLYBAND is not a 'discovery', except in so far as his lively picture of ordinary Elizabethan citizens at home and of their children at school comes as a surprise to the reader who happens upon it unexpectedly. The delight of that original encounter remains, however far the range of our studies may afterwards take us; and the sensation of discovery with which his dialogues first impinge on the mind continues to please, even when we have realized that the history of education has long since placed him and given him his due. For the social historian as for the ordinary reader he has that real touch of Main Street veracity which gets under the skin of the normal; and he uses it more effectively than the so-called realists of the time, whose relish in general is not for the dailyness of life so much as for the extravagant humours of the English eccentric thrown up by the middle and lower classes. Admittedly, Holyband is not literature and not a discovery, but he is incidentally very good fun, and he is certainly very good value to all who seek a greater intimacy of understanding of the ordinary as a basis for their own discovery of the temper of this great age.

There is a considerable amount of information available about Claudius Holyband, who for some thirty years taught French in Elizabethan London; but of Claude De Sainliens, *gentilhomme bourbonnais,* born at Moulins, we know nothing. He arrives upon the English scene 'from the dominion of the King of France', and the patent roll (8 Eliz. p. 6, m. 36.)

which grants him letters of denization on 14 January 1566 lists him as 'A Sancto Vinculo, Claud'. When he appears for the first time in the Returns of Aliens for the City of Westminster in 1568 he has anglicized himself as 'Claudius Hollybarne scolemaster, denizen', who goes to 'the parishe churche of St Margarettes', and with his usher, one John Henrycke, is described as 'French persones ij'.[1] After this his name appears from time to time in similar records, thanks to the efficient Tudor regulations which dealt with the contemporary refugee problem, caught up the alien immigrant in its registration machinery, naturalized him—if he was lucky—or gave him denizen rights, taxed him and generally kept a watchful eye upon his activities, his place of residence and even his church-going. Only one of these official records, however, links him with his past—namely, the 1571 Returns of Aliens which enters him as 'Glood Holibrand' and adds the helpful note, 'hath byne here vij yeres'.[2] Of his origins, that is to say, we know nothing beyond his name, nationality, birthplace and probable date of arrival in this country. We infer, from English documents and from what he tells us in his books, that he was a Huguenot refugee and that he came to London, probably with a wife and two children, sometime between 1564 and the end of 1565. Moulins, his native place, was a Protestant stronghold. In 1562, and again in 1565–6, severe measures were taken to clear the town of the Reformers, and from the date of his denization it seems probable that De Sainliens, having been fortunate enough to escape with his life in the first of these persecutions, fled to England when in

[1] *Huguenot Soc. Publ.* x, iii, 400.
[2] *Ibid.* p. 471.

December 1565 Charles IX and Catherine de Médicis arrived in person to deal with these obstinate heretics.

In her Paris doctorate study, *Un Devancier de Cotgrave: La vie et les œuvres de Claude De Sainliens* (Paris, 1908), Miss L. E. Farrer gives a full account of Holyband's life and analyses minutely his phonology, grammar and lexicography.[1] Here it must suffice to say that he prospered as a schoolmaster in London: that he found noble patronage, as did many of his fellow-exiles: that he took to himself an English wife—one Anne Smith—when he remarried in 1578: that he planned and achieved a comprehensive work on the French language in four parts,[2] and produced some other texts for the teaching of French and Italian; and in 1597 was still teaching French at his school in Paul's Churchyard at the sign of the Golden Ball. No subsequent records of himself or his family have been traced, and his ultimate fate is unknown.

Just as it is possible to connect the approximate date of his arrival in England with the historical circumstances of Huguenot persecution at Moulins in the 1560's, so, perhaps,

[1] For the purposes of ordinary reference a summary of his life can be found in the present writer's *The Elizabethan Home Discovered in Two Dialogues* (1949 ed.). Miss K. Lambley devotes considerable attention to his work in her chapters on the Protestant refugee teachers in *The Teaching and Cultivation of the French Language in England during Tudor and Stuart Times* (1920). Her book gives a remarkably detailed and fascinating account of the development of French studies in England: it is also full of human interest, and provides the historical, social and linguistic background against which an individual achievement like Holyband's must be considered. The original elements in his teaching of grammar had been discussed last century, first by Charles Livet in *La grammaire française et les grammairiens au xvi⁰ siècle* (Paris, 1859) and later by Thurot in *De la prononciation française depuis le commencement du xvi⁰ siècle* (Paris, 1881).

[2] See Appendix C.

it is not unreasonable to accept Miss Farrer's tentative sugges-
tion that the total disappearance of his name from English
records after 1597 may be connected with another and more
important event in French history, namely the Edict of
Nantes in 1598. As persecution drove him from France so its
cessation and the Protestant triumph may have enabled him
to return from his long exile. Miss Farrer has traced the name
De Sainliens, in various forms, in early sixteenth- and then in
seventeenth-century records connected with Moulins and the
district. It would be pleasant to think that after half a lifetime
of schoolmastering in a foreign land the end of the century saw
Holyband translated back to his native condition of *gentil-
homme bourbonnais*. 'Let us hope that this was the case',
writes A. W. Pollard, 'and if so, that Anne Smith of the City
of London had learnt to speak French and to appreciate French
cooking.'

Were there but space enough and time it would be no
unprofitable exercise to inquire into the degree of intimacy of
the social relationships implied by Holyband's dedications and
by the commendatory verses written for him by men like
Richard Mulcaster or George Gascoigne. The link with the
former would presumably be professional, with the latter
further to seek. His dedications start off in very good society,
with the heir of the Sackvilles as the nominal and his father as
the actual patron of his first book and also its successor, *The
French Littelton*; and within a few years his repute—or his
connexions—enabled him to aspire to the dignity of royal
patronage for his *De Pronuntiatione*.[1] But of more associative
interest than any, perhaps, is the dedication of his 1583 *Campo*

---

[1] See Appendix C.

di Fior to 'the yong gentle-woman Mistris Luce Harington', daughter to Master John Harington Esquire. This is no other than the renowned Lucy Harington, afterwards Countess of Bedford, wife of Edward Russell, the third Earl, friend and patroness of so many of the outstanding poets of the time— among them Chapman, Daniel, Donne, Drayton, Ben Jonson. Her father was created Lord Harington of Exton at James I's coronation, and he and his wife became the official guardians of the Princess Elizabeth: in after years, to Elizabeth of Bohemia, 'Queen of Hearts', Lucy, a dearly-prized and loyal friend, was to be her 'deare Bedford'. Lucy was a Lady of the Privy Chamber and a brilliant figure at the court of Anne of Denmark. Many of the writers of the time dedicated their poems or books to her: Daniel invoked her as 'learned Lady', and Donne as 'God's masterpiece'; but it is unlikely that we shall find an earlier tribute than Holyband's, when at most she was a child of two. It was, of course, intended as a compliment to her 'most vertuous parents', which is rendered all the prettier by the fact that her mother Anne, daughter and heir of Sir Robert Kelway, had been one of his pupils and that in November 1580, apparently upon the occasion of her marriage, he had dedicated to this 'très-sage et très-vertueuse damoiselle' his *Treasurie of the French tong* and his *Treatise for Declining of Verbes*.[1] And so, with one dedication leading to another, we come to the link which connects the French refugee schoolmaster and Lucy Harington, destined to become

[1] Lucy was the eldest child, but the date of her birth is not known. She married Edward Russell, then aged twenty-two, on 12 December 1594. *G.E.C.* gives the date of John Harington's marriage to Anne Kelway as 'before 6 March 1581', but these two dedications of 5 and 15 November 1580 enable us to put it back by at least four months, possibly more.

one of the most cultured and remarkable women of her time—
a link which constitutes one of the toughest strands in the
Elizabethan fabric and is something quite vital to our understanding of its quality, namely the absolute importance given
in life to religious belief. The guardians of the Protestant
Princess were themselves the staunchest of Protestants: to
Holyband John Harington is 'ce Gonfanon et parangon de
toute gentilesse' who in marrying Anne Kelway 'a vrayement
choisi parti digne de soy' and chosen as one would expect of
a man of his piety and integrity of life and his 'zele très-ardent
envers la vraye religion'. We shall end where we began, in
all probability, whenever we seek reasons for any particular
acquaintance or patronage. The Sackville connexion was
Protestant: at the other end of the social scale we find as one
of his adult pupils the playwright and pageant-poet, Anthony
Munday, anti-Catholic pamphleteer, spy and informer.
Holyband came to England as a Huguenot refugee, and if he
ever returned to France the one thing we may quite certainly
assume is that he ended his days in the faith for which he had
endured a thirty-year exile. Patronage could mean both
influence and financial rewards, and Holyband could hardly
have been indifferent to either, but in 1580 and 1583 neither
he nor his patrons could possibly have foreseen the brilliant
Harington future: John was not knighted until 1584 and did
not succeed his father, Sir James Harington of Exton, until
1592. The fundamental connexion was the 'zele très-ardent' and
'la vraye religion', coupled, as he says in his dedication to Lucy,
when speaking of her parents, with 'the good will they beare to
learning and the earnest inclination they have to bring you up in
such vertuous exercise as is most meete for your tender yeares'.

Holyband's faith determined the main course of his life and by so doing gave him a cause which harnessed the main energy of his mind. Like others of his compatriots he could have earned an easy enough living, teaching well or indifferently, or, as he says everyone does, 'after his own fantsie': in which case he would have left behind him as little memorial as they have done. But Holyband, who told the two-year-old Lucy Harington, 'sweete be the frutes which do spring out of the knowledge of tongues', was a man who loved learning for its own sake and cared with a real passion for his own language; and the task he set himself, in consequence, was nothing less than the general reform of the methods of French teaching so that the Englishman might become the perfect French scholar and appreciate to the full the beauties of the language and its literature. He knew the Englishman's difficulties—none better: his natural trouble with the pronunciation, for example, or with the conjugating of verbs, which was always, as he reminds Anne Harington, 'à vous et à tous mes aultres escholiers tant fascheuse'. But into 'what a world of profit and delight' could he not lead these same 'escholiers'! *Sir, how do you teach your scholars, considering that they do speak French as naturally as if they were born in France? I do teach them first to read well and perfectly....* First, mastery of reading and the correct pronunciation, with the rules of pronunciation, grammar and syntax, for 'th'unlearned': then, those so vexatious verbs—a treatise to themselves: then, 'a frenche and englishe Dictionarie beautified with divers and fitte phrases'—mastery of words and their subtleties, a copious vocabulary: finally, 'for the learned in the Latin tongue', a conspectus of modern scholarship, theory, controversy, pronunciation and orthography—a rationale of his whole procedure and method. It was indeed bravely planned: what is more, the plan was carried out and the four parts all published within five years,[1] though something nearer ten probably went to their making. And now only the *Littelton*, for 'th'unlearned', is allowed its historical value. Modern comment has dismissed the vexatious *Verbs* as a trifling affair. The *Dictionarie* was appropriated by Cotgrave as basic treasure trove, and has passed as his ever since. The *De Pronuntiatione* probably missed its market even in its own day: mercifully, it is in Latin....No doubt Holyband was at his best in his own classroom: no doubt. But what a project!

Though it had no regular place in the grammar school curriculum, French was a popular subject in Elizabethan England, as it had been, indeed, for the nobility and those aspiring to high office in the state throughout the Tudor period. Alone among the modern tongues it shared with Latin the status of a universal language, in which scholars and diplomats, gentlemen and princes might be expected to converse and even to correspond. At a lower level, too, the practical value of being able to speak and understand some French, if not to read and write it, was well recognized by all merchants and traders who had business in foreign parts. The services of French tutors, both English and foreign, had long been in request at court and in noble families, and numbers of the refugees driven from France and the Low Countries by religious persecution found employ-

---

[1] Reckoning, that is, from the *Littelton* of 1576 (cf. Appendix A), and disregarding the *Schoolemaister* or treating it as a preliminary experiment, which for the purpose of the *magnum opus* was replaced by the *Littelton*.

ment of this kind. By the latter half of the century, however, the demand for French tuition had become so much more general that it encouraged some of these exiles to set up private schools, not only in London but in towns such as Canterbury, Southampton, Rye and Norwich. These schools catered, apparently, for the children of well-to-do citizens of the middle class who would normally have sent their sons to the free grammar schools but were prepared to afford fees to secure tuition in this useful 'extra'.

There are no contemporary accounts of these French schools unless we assume that Holyband provides us with a substantially true picture in the dialogue *Of Scholers and Schoole* which appeared in *The French Littelton* in 1576.[1] In it he has admittedly taken hints from the schoolboy scenes in the Latin dialogues of Vives, but he so obviously adds little details and utilizes his own experience to make the whole thing more English and more topical and alive, that it is reasonable to regard it as authentic and genuinely informative.

The picture that emerges is delightfully vivid and entertaining. The school was expensive, with its charge of a shilling a week or fifty shillings a year,[2] compared with, say, the Merchant Taylors' where even the richest paid no more than twenty shillings a year, or with Shrewsbury where education was free to all and a burgess paid only a fourpenny admission fee for his son. But it gave value for money in the shape of an eight-hour school-day, and besides following the normal grammar school curriculum in Latin and using the same texts, it also gave elementary instruction on the preparatory or

[1] See Appendix A for the problem of the date of the first edition.
[2] In 1573, at Lewisham, he had only charged forty shillings.

'petty school' level, teaching its youngest pupils to read and write and also 'to cipher' (*chiffrer*, i.e. the rules of elementary arithmetic). To Latin it devoted the shorter morning session, from eight o'clock to eleven: the afternoon, from twelve to five, was given to French; and it is interesting to note that the first exercise the pupils are given when they reassemble is the famous 'double translation'—first, French into English and then English into French. At eleven, after prayers, the pupils were sent home for the dinner hour, and at five, after evening prayers, they were dismissed with an admonition to 'rehearse' (*répéter*) their homework six or seven times after supper, so as to be able to learn their lesson quickly the next morning.

In 1573 Holyband, according to his earliest book, *The French Schoolemaister*, was keeping a school of this kind 'at Lewsham hard by the Church'. In 1576 he appears again in London records as a 'stranger' residing in Salisbury Court, the home of Lord Buckhurst, and according to his *Arnalt and Lucenda* (1575) and *The French Littelton* had set up a school 'in Paules Churcheyard hard by the signe of the Lucrece'—that is, next door to the printing house of Thomas Purfoote. According to the title-page of his *Treatise for Declining of Verbes* he had moved to his third and last school address, 'at the signe of the Golden Ball', by 1580. At no time does he appear to have lived on his school premises, and there is nothing to tell us whether he taught his adult pupils in his classroom after school hours or at home.

On his earliest title-page Holyband calls himself 'professor of the Latin, Frenche and Englishe tongues'. Whether the young De Sainliens had already commenced schoolmaster, or had lived as *gentilhomme bourbonnais* we do not know: one thing, however, is quite certain—Claudius Holyband was first and foremost a born teacher. He was a good writer up to a point and for his own purposes, but the real gift which he brought to English school education in the last three decades of the sixteenth century was a practical and simplified method of teaching language. He was not a complete innovator, in that separably not one of his ideas was wholly new to teaching practice; but his method of combining them and the way in which he used them in the classroom and presented them in his books was his own. What distinguished him, and apparently made him the most popular of the refugee French teachers, was his practical skill in starting his pupils off quickly by 'direct' methods, so that from the beginning they learnt to pronounce correctly and by reading aloud were taught to relate the actual spoken sounds to the received spelling of the language. At the same time they were given a natural, if not systematic, grounding in grammar, by taking the rules as and when they were brought up by their reading and conversation. Taken in this way, instead of being learnt by heart as a solid body of facts, his grammar rules were bound to remain somewhat chaotic and haphazardly chosen; but as Holyband saw it, the essential thing was to get the progressive stages in the teaching process handled in the right order, and also to persuade the self-taught to approach their task from the same angle. For this purpose the existing text-books were unsuitable, 'thornie and unapte' as he calls them—hence his decision to compile his own.

The best book of the century—even if it had been easily obtainable—was far above the heads of beginners. John

Palsgrave's *L'Esclarcissement de la langue françoyse* (1530) was a learned work of a thousand pages, written for scholars— 'the first systematized attempt', as Miss Lambley says, 'to formulate rules for the French language, or indeed for any modern tongue.' At the other extreme there were popular little books, on conversation-manual lines, which provided useful phrases for everyday needs but aimed at nothing more than fluent speech on simple levels and the acquisition of a suitable vocabulary. Grammar and rules, the why and when of idiom and usage, had no place in this 'commercial' French: what mattered was to be able to make oneself understood when buying and selling, or asking for food and drink and accommodation on one's travels. No attempt was made to deal with correct pronunciation, the general opinion being that this could only be learnt by converse with Frenchmen. Between these extremes there was a smaller and more practical grammar than Palsgrave's in *An Introductorie for to lerne to rede, to pronunce and to speke French trewly* (? 1534), by Giles Duwes who had been tutor to all Henry VII's children and later to the Princess Mary. Duwes' insistence that practice in speaking and the acquisition of a good vocabulary should come before the mastering of grammatical rules must have appealed to Holyband; but during the forty and more years which separated him from these great predecessors the French language and linguistic studies had developed in such a way that neither of them was sufficiently up-to-date for Holyband's purposes. For ordinary use his text-books superseded theirs during the last quarter of the century, and we shall perhaps do greater justice to his practical ability and his definite if modest achievement if we realize that he himself went on being reprinted and was not finally superseded until after 1668—a time-lag in teaching practice which would have shocked him profoundly.

In his efforts to restore a pure French pronunciation and to enable his pupils to read any French book, Holyband faced an accumulation of difficulties. He himself spoke the purest French—that of Tours, Orléans, Bourges. The natural roughness of English sounds as against the smoothness of the French was an initial difficulty, as was the English tendency to place the stress on the wrong syllable; and in the period which stretched between Palsgrave and Holyband the general acceptance of an anglicized pronunciation both for French and Latin had made matters worse. The corruption was carried a stage further by the steady influx of religious refugees speaking every variety of French dialect or provincial accent: too many of his fellow-teachers came from the Low Countries, Normandy, Hainault, Burgundy, and passed on recognizable tricks of speech against which he was always warning his own pupils, as for instance the Fleming or Walloon pronunciation of *c* as the French *ch* or English *sh*—*shela* for *cela*. To complicate the matter still further, when it came to reading or text-book work, the French grammarians who had been working upon spelling and phonetics had launched the struggle between the old orthography and the reformed method which sought to discard superfluous letters and to phoneticize.

Much as he favoured simplification and desirous as he was to indicate sounds by spelling, Holyband could not bring himself to adopt the phonetics of the reformers, mainly because such spellings disguised or destroyed both the etymology of words and the true quantities of syllables. There was, moreover, the practical problem: French books used orthodox spelling, so that if the English student mastered only the phonetic spelling he would find himself sadly at a loss when he turned to the reading of French literature. Holyband solved his problem by a compromise and invented a system of his own. His chief device was to mark with a cross all letters which were not to be sounded, and he assures us that the practice afforded by working through his book was sufficient to enable his pupils to know at sight when reading an unmarked book which letters were silent and which had to be pronounced. He makes a further concession to reform by writing *k* for *qu*:[1] also *s* between vowels as *z* 'for the onely ease of English men'. Other similar 'easements' creep into his text occasionally, but not consistently, as *tans* for *temps*, and the modern *l'école* for *l'eschole*. In the main, however, he keeps the phonetic spellings in the place where he felt they were most useful—that is, in the explanatory rules for pronunciation. According to himself his method was so successful that if a new scholar arrived from another French school who mispronounced any letter, his own pupils could 'spie the fault as soone as I'; and, what is more, could identify the particular local accent of the master who had taught him.

Holyband sought to teach his pupils 'the true phrase of the language', its natural rhythmic movement, its transitions and elisions, its 'perfect annexinge of syllables, wordes and sentences'. The modern reader must judge for himself how successfully he thinks he could 'frame his tongue' by the Holyband methods, but if he will try the sounds according to instructions he will realize that he had a fine, sensitive ear.

[1] In this, Miss Farrer suggests, he may have been following De Baif: he was an admirer of the Pléiade.

As Miss Farrer points out, in discussing the qualities of the vowel *e* he anticipates all that modern knowledge assigns to it: 'le timbre: fermé et ouvert, aigu ou moins aigu (il n'emploie pas le mot grave); 2° la durée: qui peut être de trois temps; 3° l'intensité: son vif ou lent et mourant; 4° la hauteur musicale: en prononçant *e* ouvert on lève la voix.' She finds him better on 'la phonétique' than grammar: his arrangement is not always clear and orderly: 'On dirait des observations recueillies au cours de l'enseignement et qui s'attachent aux principales difficultés de ses élèves anglais.' His *phonétique* is not a complete body of doctrine, and she would have liked him to have given more attention to the diphthongs, but all the same 'il montre la voie aux modernes dans ses efforts pour décrire le mouvement des organes en produisant les sons *u, l, ñ*'.

Such, in briefest outline, was the nature of the endeavour of which *The French Schoolemaister* and *The French Littelton* were born. He chose their titles very cleverly. Name and date at once associate the former with Roger Ascham's famous book *The Scholemaster* (1570). The link was obviously intentional as the book is dedicated to 'the Worshipful and towardly yonge Gentilman Maister Robert Sackville', the problem of whose education had originally inspired Ascham's treatise. It was a successful bid for the patronage of Master Robert's father, Thomas Sackville, part-author of *Gorboduc*, author of the *Induction* and Buckingham's lament in *The Mirrour for Magistrates*: three years later, when he dedicated the *Littelton* to the same towardly young gentleman, Holyband was actually living in Salisbury Court, the Sackville mansion.[1]

---

[1] There is no evidence to show that he was acting as tutor to Master Robert or any of his brothers and sisters. He was not teaching him in or

The title of the second was perhaps an even happier inspiration. As every law student began his grounding with Littleton's *Tenures*, 'so euery person purposing to haue anie understanding of the French tongue, might (for his first labour, and as his readiest way to come to the knowledge of the ground of the same tongue) begin with this present book'. In the original edition he explains that 'according to the counsaile of that worthy gentilman, Master Onsley, Warden of the Fleete', he has 'caused it to be printed in this small volume, that it might be easier to be caried by any man about him'. It makes a pretty little book for the pocket, two inches by four; and evidently Master Onsley knew what he was talking about, as successive editions remained practically the same size.

The material of these two books is substantially the same. In one sense, the *Littelton* is merely a revised edition—a second attempt to do the same thing, only to do it much better. Nevertheless, they appear to have gone on competing with each other, on almost equal terms, for well over half a century. The *Schoolemaister* describes itself as 'set forthe for the furtherance of all those whiche doo studie priuatly in their owne study or houses'; but it is not, in fact, a book which the self-taught would find easier to use than the *Littelton*, and there is nothing to show that this distinction without difference influenced their comparative popularity. How many editions of each were published I should not like to say: printed lists

before 1573, as Robert, aged twelve, was then at Oxford, and Holyband explicitly states that he is dedicating the *Schoolemaister* to him 'because you are not entred any thinge at all into the language but are new to learne'. Cf. Appendix A.

give a total of fifteen *Schoolemaisters* between 1573 and 1668, and fifteen *Litteltons* between 1576 and 1639.[1] For his best picture of Elizabethan life we must turn to the former; but if we consider his achievements as teacher and grammarian as seriously as they deserve we realize that the *Littelton* is the better book. He himself regarded it as the more important, and he revised every edition and kept it up to date until he disappeared from London life in 1597. If any one of his books is to be made available in what is virtually a facsimile reprint it is right for the *Littelton* to be thus singled out, and equally proper that an edition showing the last traces of the author's revising hand should be used, rather than the first.[2]

Between the *Schoolemaister* and the *Littelton* there is, in Miss Farrer's opinion, 'un pas énorme'. As Holyband himself puts it, in the first he 'gathered and framed confusedly': then, realizing its faults, in the second 'devised an apter method and easier way'. Whereas in the first he began like Palsgrave

[1] Miss Farrer lists only those copies she has examined: Miss Lambley adds two *Schoolemaisters* and four *Litteltons*: Hazlitt and Lowndes add one each of the first, and Stengel one of the first and two of the second. It would be unsound to base estimates of their relative merits in the eyes of their contemporaries upon these figures, if only because after 1597 the *Schoolemaister* was 'newly corrected and amended', first by Peter Erondelle and then by James Giffard, who did their editing by incorporating material from the *Littelton*. Miss Lambley tells us that the *Schoolemaister* was still being advertised for sale by Thomas Passenger at the Three Bibles on London Bridge as late as 1677, and that by the end of the century it begins to appear in almost all the sale catalogues of private libraries.

[2] The present text has been set up from a copy, in the Library of Emmanuel College, Cambridge, of the eighth (1609) edition recorded in the *Short-Title Catalogue*. As far as I know the book has not been reprinted, at any rate in England, since 1630, according to Miss Farrer, or 1639 according to Miss Lambley. In *The Elizabethan Home* I have reprinted only from the dialogue portion (1925, 1930, 1949).

and Duwes with the rules of grammar and pronunciation, in
the *Littelton* he plunges his learner straight into speech, into
the dialogues: rules and explanations[1] are to be taken only 'as
occasion requireth'—that is, when they arise in connexion
with actual examples. If the pupil is to learn quickly he 'must
not entangle himself at the first brunt with the rules of the
pronunciation'; instead, let him read them over once and then
'take in hand these Dialogues' and 'first frame his tongue by
the reading'. He is, in fact, to proceed by the conversational
method, and the book is arranged so as to encourage him to
tackle the language in this way.

In the first edition of the *Schoolemaister* Holyband had not
yet evolved his system of marking silent letters: in the *Littelton*,
as we see in this reprint, he marks them with a small cross; and
in later editions of the *Schoolemaister* he used a small dot. In
the matter of their respective vocabularies, however, the
earlier book has the advantage: short of a real dictionary, it
would be hard to imagine a better, and the *Littelton's*, by
comparison, seems very meagre and inadequate. In the
former, which occupies a hundred pages, he provides for all
conceivable everyday needs, ranging from heaven to hell and
from the seven deadly sins to the seven days of the week, in-
cluding by the way the birds of the air, the beasts of the field,
the earth and its inhabitants, their countries and cities, their
clothing, their trades, their professions, and, of course, the
usual list of the members of the body with which Alice and the
Princess Katharine make such pretty play in *Henry V*. It is
possible that he cut down the *Littelton* to a twelve-page
vocabulary because he had by then decided to compile

[1] 'Set (for a purpose) at the latter end of this booke': original edition.

a separate dictionary and had already started on his *Treasurie of the French tong* (see Appendix C). The *Littelton*, on the other hand, devotes much more detailed attention to pronunciation, and the *Schoolemaister* does not provide any continuous text like the *Littelton*'s twenty-page *Traicté des Danses* to give the learner practice in reading.[1]

To appreciate fully both the novelty and the orthodoxy of Holyband's methods the non-specialist must consult Miss Farrer's very detailed study. For the social historian and the ordinary reader the main attraction of these two text-books will always be his Dialogues, and it was good salesmanship on his part to keep one long first-rate specimen peculiar to each. The use of this form was, of course, not new to language textbooks: together with collections of everyday phrases, short dialogues are to be found in the Latin conversation-manuals from the late fourteenth century on, and in the early French specimens such as Caxton's *Dialogues in French and English* (*c.* 1483) and the Pynson-Wynkyn de Worde *Lytell treatyse for to lerne Englisshe and Frensshe* (*c.* 1498). Holyband had also been anticipated in 1553 by a fellow-countryman, Peter du Ploiche, whose little text-book, *A treatise in English and Frenche...right necessary and profitable for al young children*, contained several 'familiar dialogues' to which he was directly indebted. There is no question of rivalry: Du Ploiche's dinner-table conversation has neither the dramatic feeling and cohesion, nor the scenic structure and the liveliness of characterization found in his successor; but as far as choice of topics and useful phrases goes, his fourth dialogue reads like rough

[1] Miss Farrer believes this may be Holyband's own work. She finds it much inferior to Lambert Daneau's work of the same name.

notes for Holyband's more imaginative and accomplished version. Even in the other dialogues, however, where the relationship is closer, du Ploiche is disjointed and crude while Holyband seems able to transform almost any group of phrases into a miniature scene and to impart little touches which instantly bring the situation and the speakers to life, as when, for example, at the end of his buying-and-selling dialogue, one of the shoppers finishes by saying to his friend, 'Let us buy some babies (*poupettes*) for our children: shall we?'

Holyband's best dialogue, and his longest, is the one in *The French Schoolemaister* (sigs. F^v–Kiij^v), in which he introduces us to the parents of his pupils—the well-to-do citizens and tradesmen of London, with their wives and servants and apprentices, their friends and relations, their homes and their City haunts, their dinner tables, their gossip, their jokes, their behaviour, their topics of conversation. It is here that he really lets himself go as a writer, and makes us fully aware what a shrewd and sympathetic observer of the English scene had arrived in our midst 'from the dominion of the King of France'. The natural flow of the talk and Holyband's own enjoyment of the occasion make the reader forget the conversation-manual to become one of the party. He was never to show to better advantage his happy knack of dashing off a lightning character-sketch in a mere snatch of conversation. He has caught admirably the atmosphere of jollity and bustle and the free and easy manners of the prosperous middle-class household. With a technique reminiscent of the early film, picture after picture is flashed upon the mind in vivid, breathless sequences, as the talk shifts momently from group to group.

His only other dialogue of comparable interest—and equally successful if due regard is had to its more limited scope—is the one *Of Scholers and Schoole*, with which in its second and all succeeding editions *The French Littelton* begins. The scene in the schoolroom in Paul's Churchyard comes to life as we read, and in some curious way even the conversation-manual's necessity of piling up synonyms and alternatives turns to glorious gain, making as it were a background of hum and buzz and chattering of noisy little boys. Not the least of its triumphs is that it still passes the exacting test of pleasing and entertaining schoolchildren; and for the adult reader it has the further attraction that with Holyband, as with Mulcaster and Ascham, we escape from the worst rigours of Elizabethan childhood and education into a more credible world. The school-day is excessively long, but nobody appears to be working with unnatural application: the master may threaten ferocious beatings, but the impression remains that in this particular classroom most of the 'little victims' were probably well able to talk themselves out of most tight corners. As we read of the pranks of John Nothingworth, who swore by God, lied twice and played by the way, or of that other young scoundrel who after the manner of his kind trod his companion's hat under foot and spat upon his paper, we recognize these irrepressibles as the fellows of those jaunty little boys who pipe up in the most unintimidated way in Shakespeare—blood-brothers to the little Macduff or the bold little Duke of York in *Richard III*.

The dialogues on travellers and inns and buying and selling are more conventional and smack somewhat of the phrase-book and the manual by comparison with these other two.

Nevertheless, the reader who in Holyband's phrase will 'take a little paine' in the reading will find pleasant, curious and entertaining trifles in each section. He will catch literary echoes, and can ponder over that heightening of apprehension which comes from the reciprocal impact of document and poetry, as when Holyband's traveller, approaching the inn, remarks to his companion, 'Truly I feare lest we be here robbed... we will spurre a little harder, for it waxeth night', and we remember

> The west yet glimmers with some streaks of day:
> Now spurs the lated traveller apace
> To gain the timely inn.

Or, if words and their changing meanings are his pleasure, he may be surprised to find that to Holyband *tizanne* (tisane) means 'barley water', and tracing it on through Cotgrave be even more surprised to find that our *Oxford English Dictionary* still agrees with the sixteenth-century Frenchman, and, ignoring our popular usage, 'an infusion of herbs', says firmly, 'barley water', and adds not a single alternative. Again, if he has not previously encountered the meal which Holyband calls 'an unchion', it may entertain him to track it down in Holyband's own dictionary and in Cotgrave under *gouster*, and so on to the *O.E.D.*, to find them all agreeing that 'a nuncheon' (or 'nonchion') is a lunch, 'an afternoon's banket' or an afternoon drinking. And if he fancies himself as a translator it will give him cause for sympathetic amusement to find that in spite of a good command of English idiom Holyband to the end of his days can do no better for *mon amie* than 'my shee-friend'. 'Sweet hart', one might have thought, would have served reasonably well in Elizabethan

England, though useless now: evidently, however, in practice an Elizabethan writer was as puzzled as we are to get a just equivalent. The not entirely frivolous question it poses may be: is Holyband merely intent here to illustrate masculine and feminine endings, and if so what mode of address did he himself use for his she-friends in ordinary conversation? 'Madam' or 'good madam' is too formal: 'dearest chuck'—in which, presumably, we are supposed to believe—is too intimate by half: 'good lady' or 'good gentlewoman' is hardly better than 'good madam': 'sweet coz' implies relationship, however slight: 'sweet lady' comes nearer the mark, or perhaps 'good mistress' or 'sweet mistress'.... It is permitted that one amuse oneself.

There are trifles, too, for the social historian—the touches that help us to visualize. One may 'know' about riding-boots, boot-hose and spurs, know what they look like in pictures, and be aware that an Elizabethan traveller at the end of his miry and dusty journey would not go about the house or the inn without first taking them off. But how many of us have taken the trouble to *watch* this everyday occurrence, to stage the scene in the mind's eye? Not the present writer, certainly, until Holyband nudged the imagination with an unexpected little bit of detail—'pull off first my bootes: make them cleane: *and then put my boot-hosen, and my spurres therein*: give me my slippers.' We do not 'know', but it is a good guess that those boot-hosen and spurs were stuffed inside the boots when they were taken away to be cleaned as well as when they were brought back to their owner.

To dwell too exclusively upon his dramatic merits, however, would be unfair to Holyband the grammarian, and especially so if it were to lead to the neglect of the rest of his work; because the further one explores the more fully does he emerge as an attractive personality. He is a friendly soul and an enthusiast. He writes almost as he must have talked to his pupils of all ages, quick to elaborate and to explain so that the English ear shall get every nuance of pronunciation or meaning. He cares for the exact understanding as for the pure speaking, of his beloved language. It is better, he declares in his *Treasurie of the French tong*, to give a circumlocutory explanation than 'a false Englishing, as dydde those which brake the Ice before, as they doe terme it'; and though he frequently apologizes for his own inadequate English, he has, in fact, a good command of the idiom: much of his apparent quaintness is due to the demands of the conversation-manual form. He cared for languages: he cared for words; and though he loved the *douceur* of the French he appreciated the vigour and homeliness of the English phrase in ordinary conversation. Inspired with a genuine missionary zeal he worked steadily on at his self-imposed task of providing Elizabethan England with the good, simple, practical and up-to-date French grammars, dictionaries and 'first readers' it had hitherto lacked; and it is infinitely to his credit that in spite of exile and of the daily drudgery of long school hours he managed somehow to keep reasonably well abreast of contemporary linguistic scholarship, and at the same time always to write with the needs and the characteristic pronunciation difficulties of the average English speaker well in mind. He illustrates the French by analogous English sounds, he helps the learner by telling him how to use tongue or palate,[1] and enforces his

[1] See, for example, 'Of two, ll.' p. 160.

advice by the homely chaff which a beginner will be likely to remember, as when, for example, he warns him of the difficulty Englishmen have with *e* feminine and recommends them to 'marke how they sound, *e*, in these English wordes, *able, sorte, concorde*, and let them so pronounce our sayd, *e*, feminine: saving that they shall not eate it up, but sound it in such a sorte that it may be heard'. The modern reader who gets his laugh out of the comic literalism of the translation 'the evening prayers of Cicile' for the Sicilian Vespers is entitled to his amusement, provided he remembers that it occurs because Holyband is expatiating on the right and wrong way to pronounce *ci* and is himself laughing at the French scholars of his own time who said 'Shishero' for Cicero, instead of following the Italian pronunciation.

It was a fitting recognition of the way the exile, the refugee, had both assimilated and been assimilated by English life that he ended up as an established institution, referred to affectionately as 'old Holiband'. Had he been able to dip into the future he would certainly have deplored the dullness of the so-called dialogues inflicted upon the child at school at the end of the nineteenth century—uninspired strings of disconnected phrases, without even the legendary silliness of 'the pen of the gardener's aunt' to mitigate boredom and stimulate parody. One could not, as we say, have cared less that a lorry (*camion*) tore away the side of the omnibus so that Charles was *blessé*: we had not been told who Charles was and where he went to school and what he did there. 'Old Holiband' could more than have held his own against any 'first reader' of that date, and of that style. Our own time pays him a double tribute. We acknowledge the debt of past generations when a University Press treats his *Littelton* as a document of genuine interest to the historian of French studies in England. But to 'old Holiband' we have given again something of that affectionate regard which is won from us not by an academic hall-mark but by personality. In all his work there was zest, gusto—an awareness of the quality of people and scenes and of the excitement and pleasure that lies in the mystery of words and the mastery of language. Scholarship acknowledges his status as grammarian; but his charm for the ordinary reader, which has taken him as far as the Antipodes where his dialogues are read and enjoyed in Australian schools, lies in his capacity to give such an eager and appreciative response to the goings-on of life in London nearly 400 years ago—a response so alert, so direct and natural and so communicative that, as of 'good old Mantuan'—to echo but to misquote Holofernes—we can say, 'He who loves thee not knows thee not.'

THE FRENCH
LITTELTON.

A MOST EASIE, PER-
FECT, AND ABSOLVTE WAY
to learne the French tongue.

Set foorth by CLAVDIVS HOLYBAND,
Gentil-homme Bourbonnois.

Dum spiro, spero.

LONDON,
Printed by Richard Field, dwelling
in the Black-Friers.
1 6 0 9.

TO THE RIGHT WORSHIPFVL AND
MOST LEARNED GENTLEMAN,
Sir William Herbert of Swanſey,
Knight.

CLAVDIVS HOLYBAND wiſheth all honour
and felicitie.

WHEN I had compiled and put to light the French
Schoolemaiſter (right Worſhipfull) I gathered and
framed therein confuſedly, and as it were at randon, certaine
rules for the learner of the French tongue: knowing not then,
to what end or ſucceſſe my labour ſhould attaine. But ſeeing
my trauell therein (contrarie to my expectation) to be liked
of, both by the Nobilitie and meane eſtate of this flouriſhing
Realme: I was thereby encouraged to proceede toward the
fulfilling of my former promiſe: namely to deuiſe and publiſh
ſome apter method and eaſier way, whereby the Engliſh
nation might know and ſee the depth of the French language:
which method and way, I haue publiſhed, by and in the name
of the French Littelton. That as euery ſtudent applying himſelfe to the knowledge of the lawes of this Realme, doth commonly trauell in the booke called Litteltons tenures, to learne
at his firſt entrie the grounds of the Law for the matter therein
handled: ſo euery perſon purpoſing to haue anie vnderſtanding
of the French tongue, might (for his firſt labour, and as his
readieſt way to come to the knowledge of the ground of the
ſame tongue) begin with this preſent booke: which I haue
cauſed to be printed in this ſmall volume, that it might be

caried more eafily by anie man about him. Wherein alfo I haue
qualified the great ftrife betweene them that would haue our
tongue written after the ancient orthographie, and thofe that
do take away manie letters as fuperfluous in writing: in fuch
fort as I haue (I truft) pleafed both the parties. The one hath
all the letters according to the old cuftome: the other hath all
thofe that he thinketh fuperabundant, marked with a fpeciall
marke: which be thefe, ạ ḅ ç ḍ ẹ f ğ ḥ ị ḷ ṇ p̃ ḍ ṣ ṭ ſ̣ x̣ ẓ. But
in what errour they are which will haue anie letters left out,
thefe reafons may fhew. Firft the orthographie fheweth the
deriuation of the diction. Secondly it ferueth for the quantitie.
Thirdly for a ful pronunciation, when the Reader hath occa-
fion to breathe, or ftop at the midft of the member or fentence.
Laft of all, for the ancient monumēts written fo manie yeares
paft, which could not be vnderftood hereafter if the writing
were altered. Now to the intent that all the ftudents of the
French tongue may yeeld vnto your Worfhip euerlafting
thankes, as well for the liking, inuention, and deuifion of this
booke, as for their inftruction in our tongue: I haue thought
good to fet here in fewe wordes, the order of their ftudies
in this language.

The yong learner, and euerie other perfon intending to
learne the fame language, forfaking all other thornie and vnapt
bookes, (as indeed there be too many at this prefent time, and
according to that faying: *Scribimus indocti doctique, poemata
paſſim*) fhall firft frame his tongue by the reading of this worke,
as his moft eafie way to profite in his ftudie therein: marking
diligently the orthographie, and the letters noted, (the reafon
why they are left, is fhewed by the rules of the pronunciation,)
that when he fhall happen on other bookes printed without

thefe characters, he may remember which letters ought to be
vttered, and which ought not. Here the cauillation of fome
ignorants preuaile but a litle, faying, that the learner is new
to feeke, when he cometh to a booke without fuch markes:
wherein meafuring other mens wits according to their owne,
they thinke that when they be from their Accidence, they be
out of countenance: but experience fheweth me daily the con-
trary: for after that my fcholers haue framed their tongue by
this booke, they are fo farre off to pronounce fuch letters which
ought not, that whē they heare any new fcholer coming to me
from other French fchooles, and pronouncing any letter otherwife thē it fhould be, they fpie the fault as foone as I, yea they
cannot abide it: and which is more, they will difcerne whether
the maifter which taught them firft, was a Burgonian, a Nor-
man, or a Houyvet.

Afterward let the learner reade halfe a fcore Chapters of
the New Teftament, becaufe it is both eafie and profitable:
then let him take in hand anie of the books of *Monfieur de
Launay,* otherwife called *Pierre Boayftuau,* as the beft and moft
eloquent writer of our tongue.

His workes be, *le Theatre du monde,* the *Tragicall Hiftories,*
and the *Prodigious Hiftories: Sleidans* Commentaries in French
be excellently tranflated: *Philip de Commines* when he is corrected, is very profitable and wife.

Thus moft humbly befeeching your good Worfhip to
accept the patronage of this my labour, I wifh vnto your
Worfhip the fulfilling of all your godly defires.

London this 25. of March, 1597.

GEORGE GASCOINE

Esquire

In Commendation of this Booke.

THe Perle of price, which Englishmē haue sought
　So farre abroad, and cost them there so deere,
Is now found out within our countrey heere,
And better cheape amongst vs may be bought.
I meane the French, that pearle of pleasant speech,
Which some sought far, & bought it with their liues:
With sicknesse some, yea some with bolts and gyues:
But all with paine, this peerelesse pearle did seech.
Now Holyband (a friendly French indeed)
Hath tane such paine, for euery English ease,
That here at home we may this language learne:
And for his paine, he craueth no more meed,
But thankful harts, to whom his pearles may please:
Oh thanke him then, that so much thank doth earne.

Tam Marti quàm Mercurio.

SONNET.

ANglois, tu as esté separé du François:
Et toy aussi, Frãçois, de l'Anglois qui t'embrasse
De langage divers, plus long temps que de Race,
Tu l'as esté de foy, & quelque temps de Lois.

Les Lois n'ont empesché, ô François, que l'Anglois
Ne t'aye ja receu, car Foy t'a mise en grace,
Foy que tous les éleuz enfans de Dieu ramasse
En un corps avec Christ, l'Eternel Roy des Roys.

Il ne reste donc plus que le divers langage,
Mais voicy Holyband, qui faict un mariage,
De tous les deux, sus donc, lisez le d'un accord.

Si qu'en langage, en race, en Foy, & Lois unis,
Viviez en double paix, de vray amour munis:
Et le monde vaincrez, peché, Satan, la mort.

                                    Pax in bello.

DIALOGVES,

OR FAMILIAR TALKES TO ENTER &
EXERCISE THE READER.

*I*F the Reader meaneth to learne our tong within a short space, *he must not entangle himselfe at the first brunt with the rules of the pronunciation: but after he hath read them ouer, let him take in hand these Dialogues: and as occasion requireth, he shall examine the rules, applying their vse vnto his purpose: as for exāple: when you read,* Dieu vouş doinţ bon jour, *you must know the cause vvhy,* s, *and,* t, *are not expressed, and the rule of tvvo consonants shevveth the reason. You knovv not how,* x, *is pronounced at the words end, secke the rule of,* x, *and it vvill be plaine: so let these tvvo examples serue for all the rest. VVhere you shall note, that the annotations which be in the margent of the French pages, are according vnto the old and ancient orthography of our tongue.*

k, *for,* qu.

Note that all vvords here vvritten vvith, k, *are through and in all other bookes printed vvith,* qu.

z, *for,* ſ.

Likevvise here I haue vvritten, z, *in the middest of the vvord, in stead of,* ſ, *for the onely ease of English men: because vve do euer sound the single,* ſ, *betvveene tvvo vowels in one vvord as,* z.

Of Scholers and Schoole.

GOd giue you goodmorrow Sir:
good morrow goſſip: good morrow my
ſhe goſſip: God giue you a
good morrow and a good yeare.
    And vnto you alſo: whither go you ſo early?
whither leade you your ſonne?
    I bring him to ſchoole, to learne
to ſpeake Latine and French:
for he hath loſt his time till now:
and you know well that it were better
to be vnborne then vntaught:
which is moſt true.
    You ſay true: it is true certainly;
But whither goeth he to ſchoole?
Jn Paules Church yard, at the
ſigne of the golden ball: there is a Frenchman,
which teacheth both the tongues:
that is the the Latine, and French:
and which doth his dutie.
    It is the chiefeſt point: for there be ſome
which be verie negligent and ſluggiſh:
and when they haue taken $\begin{cases} readie\ money, \\ money\ before\ hand, \end{cases}$
they care not verie much,
if their ſcholers profit or no.

Des Efcholiers & Efchole.

Dieu vouȿ doinṭ bon jour Monſieur:
  bon jour compère: bon jour   *compere*
commère: Dieu vouȿ doinṭ
bon jour eṭ bon an.

    Eṭ à vous auſſi: où allez vous ſi matin?
où menez vouȿ voſtre fiḻz?

    Je le conduy à l'école, pour apprendrę   *l'efchole*
à parler Latin eṭ François:
car il a perdu ſon tans, juskes à preſent: *temps*
                                                 jufques
eṭ vous ſçavez bien kil vauḻdroiṭ mieuḻx   *quil*
n'eſtre poinṭ né, ke de n'eſtre point   *nay*
enſeigné: ce ki eſt treſ⏝veritable.   *qui*

    Vouȿ diteȿ vray: il eſṭ vray certes:
mais où va-il à l'eſcḫole?   *vati*

    Au cymitiere de Sąinṭ Paul, à l'enſeigne
de la boule d'or: il y a là un François,
ki enſeigne lèȿ deuȶ langues:
aſſavoit la Latine, eṭ la Françoiſe:
eȿ ki faiṭ ſon devoir.   *debvoir*

    C'eſṭ le principal: car il y en a   *c'eſt*
ki ſonṭ forṭ negligens eṭ pareſſeux:

eṭ kand ils onṭ prins argenṭ { contant,
                              { deuanṭ la mąin,
ilz ne ſe ſoucienṭ paȿ bęaucoup,
ſi leurs eſcḫolierȿ profitenṭ ou non.

They be folke of an euill conſcience.
the ſame is a kinde of theft.

Who doubteth of it? what is his name?
I cannot tell truly: I haue forgotten it.
Iohn, how is thy maiſter called?

He is called M. Claudius Holyband.
Is he maried? what countreyman is he?
He is a Frenchman: he hath a wife and children.
God ſaue you Sir.
Sir, God giue you a good and long life.
You take great paine with thoſe children.
There is no remedie: one muſt take paine

to get { *our liuing.*

It is well done: I haue brought here vnto
you my ſonne: praying you to take ſome
paines to teach him, that he may learne
to ſpeake French, reade and write.

J will do all that lyeth in me,
as well to acquite me of my charge,
as for mine honeſtie and praiſe.

You ſay well: what take you by the { *weeke?*
moneth?
quarter?
yeare?

A ſhilling a weeke: a crowne, a noble a moneth:
a riall a quarter: fiftie ſhillings a yeare.

It is too much: you are too deare.
If it be too much, abate of it: but I
tell you one thing, that if your ſonne learne well

Ce ſonţ genş de mauvaize conſcience: *maulvaiſe*
cela eſţ comme unę eſpèce de larcin.
  Ki en doute? commenţ s'appelle-il?   *doubte*
  Ie ne ſé certes, je lé oublié.   *ſçay, l'ay*
  Ian, commenţ s'appelle ton maiſtre?   *Jehan*
  Il s'appelle M. Claude de Sąinliens.
  Eſţ il marié? de kel païs eſt il?   *quel*
  Il eſţ François: il a famę eţ enfans.   *femme*
  Dieu vouş gard' Monſieur.
  Monſ. Dieu vouş doinţ bonne vię eţ longue.
  Vouš prenez granḑ peinę après cèş enfans.
  Il n'y a remède: il fauļt prendre peine

pour gaiǧner $\begin{cases} \text{lèş deſpens,} \\ \text{noſtre víe.} \end{cases}$

  C'eſţ bien fait: je vous é icy amené   *faiɕt, ay*
mon fiļz, vouş prianţ de prendrę un peu
de peinę à l'enſeiǧner, à fin kil apprennę   *qu'il*
à parler François, eţ lirę eţ écrire.   *eſcripre*
  Ie feré touţ ce kil me ſera poſſible,   *feray*
tanţ pour m'akiter de ma charge,   *acquiter*
ke pour mon ḩonneur eţ louänge.

                                                 que
                          $\begin{cases} \text{ſemaine?} \\ \text{mois?} \\ \text{kartier?} \\ \text{an?} \end{cases}$ *ſepmaine*

Vouş diteş bien: ke prenez vouş par   *quartier*

  Vn ſou la ſemaine: un eſcu, un noble le mois: *ſol*
un real le kartier: cinkante ſous l'an.   *ſolz*
  C'eſţ trop, vous eſteş troɓ chèr.
Si c'eſţ trop, rabbattez en: mais je vouş
diré une choſe, ke ſi voſtre fiļz apprenḑ bien, *diray*

it is not too much: but if he learne nothing,
though I should teach him for a groate a
moneth, it would be too deare for you and him.

    Call me that boy which is there at the corner:
Gabriel, haue you bene long here?
how long haue you bene here?

    About halfe a yeare Sir: a monethe
a fortnight: a seuenight: a yeare.

Can you speake
Do you speake good
⎰ *French?*
⎱ *Latine?*
   English?
   Italian?
   Spanish?
   High Dutch?
   Scottish?

    Yea Sir: a little Sir:
so, so: not verie good yet.

    VVhat booke readeth your master vnto you?

    As his scholers are fit for:
vnto some he readeth Terence, Virgil,
Horace, Tullies Offices: vnto others
Cato, Pueriles, their Accidences,
their Grammer, according to their capacitie:
as for me, I learne onely French,
to reade and write: and sometime to cipher.

    Master Holyband,
looke somewhat narrowly to my sonne:

he is somewhat hard of
⎰ *wit,*
⎱ *vnderstanding,*
   memorie:

ce n'eſt paſ trop: mais s'il n'apprenḑ rien,
encor ke je l'enſeignaſſe pour un groſ le   que
mois, ce ſeroit troṗ chér pour vous eṭ luy.

    Appeleẓ moé ce garçon ki eſt là au coin: moy
    Gabriel, aveẓ vous eſté lonǧ tans icy?   loing
temps
combien aveẓ vous icy eſté?

    Environ demy an Monſieur: un mois:
kinze jours: ḫuiçṭ jours: un an.   quinze

Sçaveẓ vouſ parler   { François?
                      Latin?
                      Anglois?
                      Italien?
Parleẓ vouſ bon   Eſpagnol?
                      Aleman?
                      Eſcoſſois?

    Ouy Monſieur: un peu Monſieur:
tellemenṭ kellement: non pas encor forṭ bon.

    Ke livre vouſ liṭ voſtre maiſtre?

    Comme ſès eſcḫoliers ſonṭ capables:
aux uns il lit Terence, Virgile,
Horace, lès Officeſ de Cicero: aux autres
Cato, Pueriles, leurs Accidens,
leur Grammaire: ſelon leur capacité:
kant à moé, j'apprens ſeulemenṭ François,   moy
à lirҽ eṭ eſcrire: eṭ aucuneᴗfois à chiffrer.

    Monſieur de Sạinliens,
regardez un peu de près à mon fiḻz:

il eſt un peu dur { d'eſprit,
                  d'entendement,
                  de memoire:

he is $\begin{cases} \textit{shamefast,} \\ \textit{wanton,} \\ \textit{wicked,} \\ \textit{a lyer, stubburne to father and} \end{cases}$
mother: correct all these faults,
and I will recompence you: hold,

$\begin{cases} \end{cases}$ I will pay you the quarter beforehand.

I thanke you: hath he a $\begin{cases} \textit{sacke?} \\ \textit{sachell?} \end{cases}$
bookes, inke, quilles and paper?

No, but I go and buy vnto him an inke-horne,

a $\begin{cases} \textit{pen-knife,} \\ \textit{and all that he hath need of.} \end{cases}$

Come hither my sonne, draw a little
neare vnto me: of what age are you?

I cannot tell maister: my father hath
put in writing the day of my natiuitie

in our Bible which is $\begin{cases} \end{cases}$ at home.

Is it in English, or in Latine? can you
reade in it? Not very well.

Go to, sit there: learne well,
to the end that you may be a good man,
and that you may do the better
seruice vnto your Prince, your countrey,
vnto the common-weale, helpe your parents,
your selfe: and all yours.

God giue me the grace and will:

il eſt ⎰ honteux,
⎱ mignard,
⎱ mauvais,
⎱ menteur, deſobeïſlant à pėrę eṭ
à mėre: corrigeẓ toutes cėṣ fautes,   *faultes*
eṭ je vouṣ recompenſeré: tenez,
⎰ je vous aḍvanceré le kartier: *quartier*
⎱ je vouṣ payeré le kartier avanṭ la mạin.
Ie vouṣ remercíe; a-ti un ⎰ ſac?
⎱ ſachet?   *a-il*
dėṣ liures, de l'ancre, plumes eṭ papier?
    Non, maiṣ je luy vay acheter un eſcritoire.   *ʋois acheptai*
⎰ canivet,
un ⎱ trenche‿plume,
⎱ ganivet: eṭ touṭ ce k'il luy faut.
Veneẓ-çà mon fiḷz, approcheẓ vous
un peu de moė: kel aagę aveẓ vous?
    Ie ne ſcé mon maiſtre: mon pėrę a mis   *ſçay*
en eſcriḅṭ le jour de ma nativité
en noſtre Bible, ki eſt ⎰ en la maiſon,
⎱ cheẓ nous.
    Eſt ellę en Anglois, ou en Latin? ſçaveẓ
vouṣ lire dedans? Non paṣ forṭ bien.
    Or ſus, ſéeẓ vouṣ là: appreneẓ bien,
à fin ke vous ſoyez un ḥomme de bien,
eṭ ke vouṣ puiſſieẓ faire meịlleur
ſervicę à voſtre Prince, à voſtre païs,
à la républike, aider voẓ parens,
vouṣ meſme: eṭ touṣ lėṣ voſtres.
    Dieu m'en doinṭ la gracę eṭ le vouloir:

make me some roome here by you.

Master, Iohn nothing-worth

hath {
sworne by God.
plaied by the waie.
sold his points.
changed his booke.
stolen a knife.
lied twice.
lost his capband.
}

Is it true? come hither companion,
you sweare: you plaie the drunkard:

vntrusse
vntie } *you.*
dispatch

Nicholas doth mocke {
me.
you.
him.
her.
them.
them.
}

Do you mocke folkes?

J will {
whippe
punish
chasten
beate
} *you:* { *He shalbe* {
beaten:
whipped:
punished:
chastened.
}

I will whip him when he is come.

It is he which plucketh me by the {
haires,
eares,
hairebush,
}

faitez moė placę icy auprėş de vous.

Mon maiſtre, Ian vau‿neant

a ⎰ juré par Dieu.
⎪ joué par le chemin.
⎪ vendu ſės égujllettes.   *eſguillettes*
⎨ changé ſon livre.
⎪ dérobé un couteau.   *deſrobé*
⎪ menti deuҳ fois.
⎱ perdu ſon cordon de bonnet.

Eſt-il vray? venez çà compagnon,
vouş jurez: vous yvrongnez:

détrouſſeҳ ⎱
détacheҳ ⎬ vous.
dépeſcheҳ ⎰

Nicolas ſe mocke de ⎰ moė.
                     ⎪ vous.
                     ⎪ luy.   *moque*
                     ⎨ elle.
                     ⎪ eux.
                     ⎱ elles.

Vouş mocqueҳ vouş dėş gens?

je vouş ⎰ feſſeré: ⎱   ⎰ batu: *feſſeray*
        ⎪ puniré: ⎬ Il fera ⎪ feſſé:
        ⎨ chaſtiré: ⎰   ⎨ puny:
        ⎱ batré: ⎱ chaſtié.

je le fouëtteré kand il ſera venu.

C'eſt luy ki me tire par lės ⎰ cheveux,
                             ⎨ oreilles,
                             ⎱ crins,

he hath giuen me $\left\{\begin{array}{l} \textit{fift,} \\ \textit{ftaffe,} \\ \textit{ftone,} \end{array}\right\}$ *vpon the head:*
a blow with the

he hath ftriken me: he hath made me bleed.
    You fhall be beaten both for companie,
for ye haue deferued it well.
    VVife, haue you fent the boy to fchoole?
haue you giuen him his breakefaft?
truly you vvill make a truant of him.
    He is not yet vp, neither awaked:
Rachel, make him rife, is it not time?
he fhould be alreadie at N:
vvhat do you there?
    I go and caufe him to rife in Gods name:
ho Francis rife, and go to fchoole:
you fhall be beaten, for it is feuen and
paft: array your felfe quickly: put you
on your knees: fay your prayers, then you
fhall haue your breakefaft: aske your fathers
bleffing: haue you faluted your father
and your mother? you forget all
ciuilitie, honeftie, all good
cuftomes, all good maners,
and learne thofe vvhich be little vvorth.
    I pray you do not tell it vnto my maifter,

and I will neuer call you $\left\{\begin{array}{l} \textit{wrinckled.} \\ \textit{hard fauoured.} \\ \textit{tooth gaper.} \\ \textit{crooke-backe.} \\ \textit{counterfeit.} \end{array}\right.$

il m'a donné $\left.\begin{array}{l}\text{poing,}\\ \text{bafton,}\\ \text{pierre,}\end{array}\right\}$ par la tefte:
un coup de

il m'a frappé; il m'a faiţ feigner.

Vouş ferez touş deux feſſez pour compagnie,
car vouş l'avez bien mérité.

Fame, avez vous envoyé le garçon à l'éſchole? *femme*
luy avez vouş baįllé ſon déjuner? *desjuner*
certeş vous en ferez un truant.

Il n'eſt pas encor levé, ny éveįllé: *eſveillé*
Rachel, faiteš le lever, n'eſt-il paş tans?
il devroiţ deſ-ja eſtrę à N: *debvroie*
ke faiteş vouş là?

Ie le vay faire lever à la bonnę ḩeure:
hau François levez vous, eţ allez à l'école: *l'eſchole*
vous ferez batu, car il eſt feþt ḩeureş
paſſées: abilleʒ vouş viſtement: metteʒ vous
à genoux: diteş voʒ priéres: puiş vous aurez
voſtre déjuner: demandeʒ la benediccion *benediction*
à voſtre père: avez vouş falué voſtre pèrę
eţ voſtre mère? vous oubliez toute
civilité, ḩonneſteté, touteş bonneş
coutumes, touteş bonneş façonş de faire, *couſtumes*
eţ apprenez celleş ki ne valenţ guères.

Ie vouş prie ne le diteş pas à mon maiſtre,

eţ je ne vous appelleré jamaiş $\left\{\begin{array}{l}\text{ridée.}\\ \text{laide.}\\ \text{édentée.}\\ \text{boſſuë.}\\ \text{contrefaite.}\end{array}\right.$

If you either ſay or do me euill,

I will cauſe you to be { *whipped:*
                              chidden:
                              beaten.

    *Peter, haue you waſhed your hands and
your face? haue you ſaid your praies, and
the Lords praier? Yea father.*

    *Tell your maiſter and miſtris
that they come to morrow to diner with me:*

and recom- { *vnto him,*
mend me   { *vnto her,*
            { *vnto them,* } *meaning* { *men,*
            { *vnto them.* }   { *women.*

    *From whence come you good ſcholer?
is it time to riſe and come to ſchoole
at nine? where haue you bene?*

    *Maiſter, J come from home: my
father hath him recommended vnto you, and*

ſendeth you { *his ring for a token,*

to the end that you beate me not.

    *That will ſerue you nothing: for you
loue not to riſe in the morning, and come to the
ſchoole betimes, as the reſt.*

    Maiſter, I met him by the way,

vvhich did { *leape:*
              { *ſlide vpon the ice:*
              { *caſt ſtones:*
              { *vvhip his top:*

Si vouş me dites ou faiteş mal,

je vouş feré { feffer,
tancer,
batre.   *feray*

Pierre, aveʒ vouş laué lêş mainş eʈ la
face? aveʒ vouş diʈ voʒ priéres, eʈ
l'oraizon Dominicale? Ouy mon père.   *l'oraiſon*

Dites à voſtre maiſtrę eʈ maiſtreſſe
kilʒ viennenʈ demain diſner avec moè: *qu'ilz*

et recommandeʒ moè à { luy,
elle,
eux,
elles.

D'où veneʒ vouş bon écholier?
eſt-il tanş de lever, eʈ venir à l'échole   *temps*
à nœuf ḥeures? où aveʒ vous eſté?

Mon maiſtre, je vienş de la maiſon: mon
père ſe recommandę à vous, eʈ

vous envoyę { ſon anneau,
ſa bague,
ſon cachet,
ſon ſiǧnet, pour enſeįgnes
afin que vouş ne me battireʒ point.

Cela ne vous ſervira de rien: car vouş
n'aimeʒ pas à lever matin, eʈ venir à l'é-
cole de bonnę ḥeure, comme lêş autres.

Mon maiſtre, je lé rencontré par le chemin,

kil { ſautoit:
gliſſoiʈ ſur la glace:
gettoiʈ lêş pierres: *qu'il*
fouëttoiʈ ſon ſabot:

vvhich did fight vvith his fift, and
balles of fnow: yea vvith all his endeuour.

I met him playing
{
  for {
    points.
    pinnes.
    cherrie ftones.
    counters.
  }
  at {
    nine pinnes.
    dice.
    cards.
    tables.
  }
}

  Come in galland: I vvill teach you
a game vvhich you know not:
and befide I vvill pay you at this time for
all your good turnes: you play vvithout leaue.

  Pardon me for this time, and I vvill do it no
more: it fhall be the firft and the laft:
Henrie Page vvill be my furetie.

  VVell, I pardon you for this prefent:
but if you do fo any more,
you fhall not be quit for the price:
I vvill pay you for all together:

John hath {
  fpitted vpon my paper.
  torne my booke and my coate.
  blotted out my theame.
  broken my girdle.
  marred my copie,
  fpoken Englifh.
  troden my hat vnder the feete
}

  Giue me the rods: ftretch your
hand: you fpeake in the nofe: you are

kil ſe battoit à couꝑs de poinǧs, eꞇ pelo-
tons de neige: voire, à touꞇe outrance:

je lé trouvé jouänt aux
{
éguillettes.
épingles.
os de cerizes.
gettons.   *j'ay*
killes.   *quilles*
dez.
cartes.
tables.
}

Entreꞃ galland: je vous enſeigneré
un jeu lekel vouꞅ ne ſçaveꞃ pas: *lequel*
eꞇ ſi vouꞅ payeré à ce coup pour touꞅ   *payeray*
voꞅ bonꞅ tours: vouꞅ jouëꞃ ſanꞅ congé.

Pardonneꞃ moe pour ſte fois, eꞇ je ne le feré   *ceſte*
plus: ce ſera la premiére eꞇ la derniére:
Henry Page ſera mon plège eꞇ caucion.

Bien, je vouꞅ pardonne pour le preſent:
mais ſi vous y retourneꞃ plus,
vouꞅ n'en ſereꞃ paꞅ kitte pour le prix: *quitte*
je vouꞅ payeré pour le tout enſemble.

Jan a
{
craché ſur mon papier:
déchiré mon livrе eꞇ mon ſayе:
effacé mon thème:
rompu ma cеinture: *Jehan*
gaſté mon example:
parlé Anglois:
foulé mon chapeau fouꞅ lèꞅ pieꝺs.   *ſoubz*
}

Baillez moè mèꞅ verges: eſtandeꞃ
la mаin: vouꞅ parleꞃ du nez: vous eſteꞅ

a ſnottie noſe: blow your noſe, and quicke.

Ah little fellow, you $\begin{cases} plaie\ the\ vice, \\ brable, \\ cakell, \\ prattle: \end{cases}$

can you conſtrue your text?

He letteth me from ſtudying my leſſon.

Haue you learned your leſſon by heart?

can you ſaie your leſſon?

Not yet Maſter.

If you miſſe at noone when I
ſhall aske you, you ſhall be whipped:
you ſhall haue foure blowes with the rod:
what is it a clocke? go ſee at the
diall, what time of the day it is.

Is is eleuen. VVhat, is it ſo late?

Yea maſter, it is time that I go, for I
ſhould be ſhent, if I ſhould tarrie anie longer.

Of whom ſhould you be chiddē, if you ſhould tarie
till twelue? who would chide you?

VVho? mine vncle, mine aunt, my grandmother.

Kneele all downe: ſay the prayers,
and get you to diner: take
heed you play not by the way:
take off your cap when you paſſe
before your betters.

come againe betime after $\begin{cases} twelue. \\ diner. \\ noone. \end{cases}$

Is it late?

morveux: mouchez vous, eṭ toſt.

Aḥ petiṭ compagnon, vouş { badinez,
babillez,
caketez,
jaſez-là?

ſçavez vouş conſtruire voſtre texte?

Il m'empeſche d'eſtudier ma leçon.

Avez vous aprinş voſtre leçon par cœur?

ſçavez vouş voſtre leçon?

Non pas encor' mon maiſtre.

Si vous y faịllez maintenanṭ kanḍ je la
vouş demanderé, vous ſerez fouëtté:
vous aurez katre coupş de fouët: *quatre*
kellę ḥeurę eſt-il? allez voir à la   *veoir*
monſtre, kellę ḥeurę il eſt.

Il eſt unzę ḥeures. Comment, eſt il ſi tard?

Ouy: il eſt tanş ke je m'en aịlle, car je ſeroyę   *ſerois*
tanſé, ſi j'attendoyę pluş longuement.

De ki feriez vouş tanſé, ſi vouş demouriez   *qui*
juskes à midy? ki vouş tanfera?   *iuſques*

Ki? mon oncle, ma tante, ma granḍ mère.

Agenouịllez vouş tous: faitez lèş priéres,
eṭ allez vous en diſner: donnez vouş
garde de jouër par lès chemins:
oſtez voſtre bonnet, kanḍ vous paſſez   *quand*
devanṭ voz majeurs:

revenez de bonnę ḥeurę aprèş { midy.
diſner.
nonne.

Eſt il tard?

It is $\left\{\begin{array}{l} \textit{twelue.} \\ \\ \\ \end{array}\right.$

   Go to, go write: where are you?
I haue no copie: make me
my pen if it pleafe you.
   VVhere be all your fellowes?
   They are not yet all come.

Sweepe the $\left\{\begin{array}{l} \textit{fchoole,} \\ \textit{fhop,} \\ \textit{houfe whileft they} \end{array}\right.$

come: where is the $\left\{\begin{array}{l} \textit{greene} \\ \textit{birchen} \end{array}\right\}$ *broome?*

take fome water to water it: for

it is verie $\left\{\begin{array}{l} \textit{duftie,} \\ \textit{dirtie,} \\ \textit{flippery,} \\ \textit{darke,} \end{array}\right.$ $\left\{\begin{array}{l} \textit{cold,} \\ \textit{hote,} \\ \textit{faire} \\ \textit{foule.} \end{array}\right.$

   Children, turne your leffons out of French
into Englifh, and then out of Englifh into French:
let vs decline a nowne and a verbe in French:
how faie you in French, N:
how call you that in French?
fay well: you fay nothing worth:
who did prompt vnto him?
   It is not I: it is Thomas.
   You lie, it is you: you fhall
pay for him, be fure thereof.

I do fee $\left\{\textit{nothing: lighten me.}\right.$

Il eſt { midy paſſé,
midy ſonné,
douze heures ſonnées.

Or ſus, allez écrire: où eſtez vous?   *eſcripre*

Ie né point d'example: taillez moè   *n'ay*
ma plume s'il vous plait.

Où ſont tous voz compagnons?

Ilz ne ſont pas encore tous venus.

Balliez { lécole,
la boutike,   *boutique*
la maizon cependant k'ilz   *maiſon*

viendront: où eſt le ballay de { geneſt?
bouleau?

prenez un peu d'eau pour arrouzer: car   *eaue*

il fait fort { poudreus, { froid,
fangeus, { chaud,
gliſſant, { beau,
obſcur, { laid.

Enfans, tournez voz leçons de François
en Anglois, et puis d'Anglois en François:
declinons un nom et un verbe en François:
comment ditez vous en François, N:
comment appelez vous cela en François?   *appellez*
dites bien: vous ne dites choſe ki vaille:
ki luy a ſouflé en l'oreille?

Ce n'eſt pas moè: c'eſt Thomas.

Vous mentez, c'eſt vous: vous
payerez pour luy, ſoyez en ſeur.

Je ne voy { goute,
rien: éclairez moè.   *eſclairez*

Go fetch fome light: light
the candell: blow out this candell,
for the tallow ftinketh; fnuffe the other:
bring the fnuffers; quickly.

I go, where be they? I cannot find them.
You can find nothing; there they be:
you haue not rehearfed your leffons,
J perceiue it well; you fhall be all
whipped to morrow morning without faile,

if you miffe therein one onely $\begin{cases} word: \\ fillable: \\ letter: \end{cases}$

if you miffe therein neuer fo little:
except you can faie it vpon your fingers end.

VVell mafter, there fhall be no fault:
fhall we faie the euening praiers?
for it is ftriken fiue.

Saie: go to fupper, without playing the
fooles by the ftreetes.

Light your $\begin{cases} lanternes. \\ torches. \\ linkes. \\ paper lanternes. \end{cases}$

God giue you good euening and good
night, and good reft, maifter.

Rehearfe after fupper the leffon which
you vvill learne to morrow morning:
and reade it fixe or feuen times: then hauing
faid your prayers, fleepe vpon it:
you fhall fee that to morrow morning

Allez kerir de la lumiére: allumez
la chandelle: fouflez ceſte chandelle,
car le fuif put: mouchez l'autre:
apportez lêſ mouchettes: viſte.
    J'y vay: où font elles? je ne lêſ peux trouver.
    Vouſ ne ſçavez rien trouver: elles ſont là:
vouſ n'avez paſ repeté voz leçons,
je l'apperçoyę bien: vous ſerez touſ
feſſez demąin au matin ſanſ nulle faute,

ſi vous y faįllez une feule ⎰parole:
                            ⎱ſyllabe:
                             lettre:

ſi vous y faįllez tant ſoit il peu:
ſi vouſ ne ſçavez ſuſ le doiğt.
    Bien mon maiſtre, il n'y aura point
de faute: dironſ nouſ lêſ priéreſ du foir?
car il eſt cinq ħeures ſonnées.
    Dites: allez fouper, et ſanſ faire lêſ
fouſ par⌣my lêſ rues.

folz

allumez voz ⎰lanternes:
             ⎱torches:
              flambeaux:
              fallots.

    Dieu vouſ doint bon foir et bonne
nuiçt, et bon repos, mon maiſtre.
    Repétez aprѐs fouper la leçon ke
vouſ voulez apprendre demąin matin:
et lifez-la fix ou fep̌t fois: puis ayant
dit voz priéres, dormez la deſſus:
vouſ verrez ke demąin au matin,

you will learne it eafily, and foone,
after you haue repeated the fame but twife.

For Trauellers.

I VVould faine haue a guide,
  to conduct vs to Paris:
for the way is dangerous, and I am
afraid that we be out of our
way: what hand fhall we take?

  Let vs fpurre hard, to ouertake that
horfeman which I do fee farre off.

  My friend, where is the right way hence
to Lyons? fhew me the way to N.
is it farre to Orleans?
how many miles haue we to S. Denis?

  Sir, it is not verie farre off, but the
vvay is verie tedious to keepe: furthermore,
it is fo dirtie and mirie, that your
horfes vvill be therein to the girths:
but J vvill teach you a nearer one
by this pathvvay: follow me.

  VVe thanke you heartilie:

haue vve not gone $\left\{ \vphantom{\begin{array}{c}a\\b\end{array}} \right.$ *aftray?*

haue J not miffed my vvay?
am J not out of my vvay?

  You are gone a little aftray?
but I vvill fet you in your right vvaie.

vouş l'aurez apprinzę aizément, et toſt: *apprinſe*
aprêş l'avoir ſeulemenţ repetée deuẋ fois.

Pour Voyagers.

JE voudroyę bien avoir une guide,   *vouldrois*
   pour nouş conduire juſques à Paris:
car le chemin eſt dangereux, eţ je   *j'ay*
peur que nous ſoyons horş noſtre
ſhemin: quelle mąin prendronş nous?   *chemin*
   Piquonş fort, afin d'attaindre ſtome   *ceſt homme*
de cheval que je voy loin d'icy.   *loing*
   Mon amy, où eſt le droiţ chemin d'icy
à Lyon? montreẕ moy le chemin de N.   *monſtrez*
eſt-il loin d'icy à Orleans?
combien de lieuës y a-il à Sąinţ Denis?
   Monſieur, il n'eſt paş forţ loin d'icy, maiş le
chemin eſt facheux à tenir: outre‿plus,
il eſt ſi fangeux & bouëux, ke voz
chevaux y feronţ juskes aux ſangles:
maiş je vous enſeigneray un pluş
court par ce ſentier icy: ſuiveẕ moy.
   Nouş vouş remercionş de bon cœur:
ne nous ſommeş nouş paş ⎰fourvoyez?
                       ⎨deſtournez?
                       ⎱eſgarez?
n'ay-je paş faįlly mon chemin?
ne ſuy-je paş horş de mon chemin?
   Vouş vous eſtes un peu détournez:
maiş je vouş remettré au droiţ chemin.   *remettray*

*J pray you leade me to the
next village, and*

I vvill giue you a
- *liard,*
- *grand blanke,*
- *ſous,*
- *teſter:*

*and yet J vvill make you drinke vvell,
vvhen vve be there arriued.*

*I am content Sir, for I am a
poore plough-man, vvhich haue loſt all
by the laſt vvarres: and am verie glad
to get a liard to buy ſome bread.*

*Go to, go before and I vvill follow you:
me thinke that I perceiue a ſteeple.*

*It is the ſame of the market towne where we go:
let me carrie your male.*

*It is not need of, for we be
arriued at the village, God be praiſed:
cauſe to draw a pint of wine: drinke:
hold, there is a peece of ſixe blanks, for
your paines, for you haue well deſerued it.*

*I thanke you Sir: ſhall I turne backe againe?
or doth it pleaſe you that I go further?
I pray thee ſet me a little in my
right way out of the village.*

*Hold at the right hand, vntill you come
to the corner of the wood, then turne at the left.*

*Haue we not theeues in the forreſt?
for that troubleth my braines.*

No ſir: for the Knight marſhall

Je vous prie conduifez moy juskes
au prochain village, et

je vous donneray un {
liard,
grand blanc,
fol,
tefton :

et fi vous feray bien boire,
quand nous ferons là arrivez.

J'en fuy content Monfieur, car je fuy
un povre labourer qui é tout perdu   *paovre*
par lés guerres paffées: et fuy bien aife
de gagner le liard pour acheter du pain.   *gaigner*

Or fus, allez devant, et je vous fuivré: *fuivray*
il me femble que j'apperçoy un clocher.

C'eft celuy du bourg où nous allons:
laiffez moy porter voftre malette.

Il n'eft de befoin, car nous fommes
arrivez au village, loué foit Dieu:
faitez tirer une pinte de vin: buvez:
tenez, voila une piéce de fix blançs, pour
voz peines, car vous l'avez bien gaigné.

Grand mercy mōfieur: m'en retourneray ie?
ou vous plait-il que j'aille plus avant?

Je te prye mets moy un peu en mon
droit chemin hors de la bourgade.

Tenez à main droite, tant que vous veniez
au coin d'un bois, alors tournez à gauche.   *coing*
                                                cefte
Ny a-il point des brigands en fte foreftz?
car c'eft ce qui me trouble le cerveau.

Non Monfieur: car le provoft dés maref-

hung the other day one
halfe dozen at that high tree,
on the gibbet which you see afore you,
at the top of the mountaine.

{ *Truly I feare leſt we be here robbed.*

No, no, feare not: all the
theeues be gone to the warres.
　　If you beleeue me, we will ſpurre
a little harder, for it waxeth night.
　　You go alreadie too faſt for me:
I am almoſt wearie: I am broken
and bruzed, as well for the way, as for
that my horſe trotteth too hard:
as for your ambling horſe, he ambleth
as eaſie, as if you were
in a boate: lend me your ſcarfe
of ſarſnet, for the duſt and
the ſunne: courage, I ſee the towne.
　　Shall we lodge at the ſuburbes, or
within the towne? where is the beſt lodging?
　　VVe muſt lie at the ſuburbes,
for they draw the drawing bridge.

Of the Inne.

M *Iſtreſſe, ſhall vve lodge here for this night?*
　My friend, ſhall I lodge here?
　　Sir, vvill you lodge me
for this night? vvill you lodge me
for my monie?

chaux en pendiţ l'autre jour une
demye douzainȩ à c'eſt haulţ arbre,
au gibeţ que voyeʐ devanţ vous,
en la cime de c'eſte montagne.

    Certeʂ jé peur que nous ſoyons icy   *i'ay*
deſtrouſſez, devalizez, aſſaſinez, vollez.

    Non non, ne craigneʐ point: touʂ lêʂ
brigans eţ volleurs ſont alléʐ à la guerre.

    Si vouʂ me croyeʐ, nouʂ piquerons
un peu pluʂ fort, car il aveſpriſt.

    Vous alleʐ deʂja troꝑ toſt pour moy:
je ſuy preſ⁓que las: je ſuy rompu
eţ briſé, tant à cauſe du chemin, que de ce
que mon cheval trotte troꝑ dur:
quant à voſtre haquenée, elle va lês
ambles auſſi aizément, que ſi vous eſtiez   *aiſement*
en un bateau: preſteʐ moy voſtre,
eſcharpe de taffetas, à cauſe de la poudrȩ
eţ du ſoleil: courage, je voy la ville.

    Logeronʂ nous auȥ fauȥ⁓bours, ou
en la ville? où eſt le meįlleur logis?

    Il nouʂ convienţ coucher auȥ fauȥ⁓bours,   *faux-bourgs*
car on lêve le ponţ⁓levis.

Du Logis.

Madame, logeronʂ nous ceans ceſte nuiçt?
Mon amy, logeray-je ceans?

    Monſieur, me vouleʐ vouʂ loger
pour ſte nuiçt? me logereʐ vouʂ   *ceſte*
pour mon argent?

Yea forsooth Sir: are you on foote
or on horsebacke? how manie are you?
　VVe be footmen: we be
on foote: we are on horsebacke:
I am neither on foote, neither a horseman: for I
am come vpon a mule: I am come by vvagon:

I am come by ⎰ *vvater:*
　　　　　　⎨ *boate:*
　　　　　　⎱ *sea, and all my companie:*
haue you a good stable? good litter?

haue you good ⎰ *hay,*
　　　　　　　⎨ *oates,*
　　　　　　　⎱ *feather beds? and*
good wine? haue you anie thing to eate?

Sir, you shall want ⎰ *nothing:*

you shall be well vsed, and your horse also:
where is the ⎰ *horse-keeper? call him to me.*

　Here I am Sir, what is your pleasure?
　Take the horse of this Gentleman,
and walke him, for feare he taketh
the glaunders: for he is verie hote: make
him a good litter: rub him well
vnder the bellie and euerie where: giue him
a bottell of hay, and a pecke of oates:
　Boy, go call me the sadler:
my horse is all galled vpon the backe:

Ouy dẹa Monſieur: eſteẹ vous à pieḍ,
ou à cheval? combien eſteẹ vous?

Nous ſommeẹ genẹ de pieḍ: nous ſommes
à pieḍ: nous ſommes à cheval:
je ne ſuy à pieḍ, ny à cheval: car je ſuy
venu ſur mule: je ſuy venu en chariot:

je ſuy venu par $\begin{cases} \text{eau:} \\ \text{bateau:} \\ \text{mer: eṭ toute ma compagníe:} \end{cases}$ *eaue*

aveẓ vouẹ bonne eſtable? bonne littiére?

aveẓ vouẹ de $\begin{cases} \text{bon foin,} \\ \text{bonnẹ avoine,} \\ \text{bon liçṭs de plume? eṭ de} \end{cases}$

bon vin? aveẓ vouẹ kelke choſe à manger?   *quelque*

Monſieur, il ne vouẹ $\begin{cases} \text{mankera rien:} \\ \text{faudra rien:} \end{cases}$

Vouẹ n'aureẓ faute de $\begin{cases} \text{rien:} \\ \text{choſe du monde:} \end{cases}$

vous ſereẓ bien traitez, eṭ voz chevaux auſſi:

où eſt le $\begin{cases} \text{valleṭ d'eſtable?} \\ \text{palefrenier? appelleẓ-le moy.} \end{cases}$

Me voy-cy Monſieur, que vouẹ plait-il?

Preneẓ le cheval de ce Gentil-ḥome,   *Gentilhome*
eṭ promeneẓ-le, de peur qu'il ne prenne
lès avives: car il eſt forṭ chauḍ: faiteẹ
luy bonne littiére: frotteẓ le bien
ſouẓ le ventrẹ eṭ par tout: baịlleẓ luy   *ſoubz*
un boteau de foin, eṭ un picotin d'avoine.

Garçon, va moy appeller le ſelier: *ſellier*
mon cheval eſt tout écorché ſur le doz: *eſchorche*

the ſaddle hurteth him vpon the ſhoulders:
the girths be broken, the croper
and the pettrell: we haue found
a verie naughtie way.

    Sir, your horſe hath no halter.

    Looke at the purſe of the ſaddle:
dreſſe him well, and I will giue you
your wine: and you ſhall haue your wine.

    There ſhall be no fault: he ſhall be well
dreſſed: hath he drunke? ſhall I water him?

    Soone, when he hath eaten a little:
then vnsaddle him, vntruſſe his taile:
and giue him two meaſures of oates.

    It ſhall be done Sir, and without fault:
doth it pleaſe you anie thing elſe?

    Bring my capcaſe: my
budget which hangeth at the ſaddlebow:
forget not my male: where is the chamber?
ſhall we taſt if the wine be good?

    Yea forſooth Sir: what wine will it pleaſe you
to drinke? ſpare not the wine.

la ſelle le blêce ſur lês eſpaules:
lês ſangles fonţ rompuës, la croupiérę
eţ le poitraįl: nous avonſ trouvé
un treſ—mauvaiſe chemin.

Monſieur, voſtre cheval n'a poinţ de licou.   *licol*

Regardez en la bourſe de la ſelle:
panſeẓ le bien, eţ je vouſ donneré   *donneray*
voſtre vin: eţ vous aureẓ voſtre vin.

Il n'y aura point de faute: il ſera bien
panſé: a il beu? l'abruveray-je?

Tantoſt, quand il aura un peu mangé:
puiſ deſſeleẓ-le, détrouſſez ſa queuë:
eţ luy baįlleẓ deuẋ meſureſ d'avoine.

Il ſera faiţ Monſieur, eţ ſanſ faute: *faiǎ*
vouſ plait-il kelke choſe d'avantage?

Apportez mon eſtuy de bonnet: ma
bougette qui pend en l'arçon de la ſelle:
n'oublieẓ paſ ma malle: où eſţ la chambre?
gouſteronſ nouſ ſi le vin eſţ bon?

Oui dẹa Monſieur: kel vin vouſ plait-il
boire? n'eſpargneẓ paſ le vin.

Donnez moy
du vin
{
blanc,
claret,
rouge,
de Rin,
de Gaſcogne,
}
{
François,
Baſtard,
cuiçt,
d'Eſpagne,
Grec.
}

apportez
moy du
{
muſcadel:
mouſt:
cidre:
peré:
}
de la
{
marvoiſie:
biére:
tizanne:
goudale.
}
    tiſanne

Margaret, bring hither a glasse,
a napkin and bread: make haste.

VVhere had you this wine? it is the
best which I haue drunke this yeare.

J went to fetch it farre off: at Master N.
at the Kings head, at Temple barre.

Do you fetch your wine so farre off?

Yea, to haue of that is good: for there is
commonly the best wine in
London: and of all sorts.

Let vs drinke well of it, whilest it is good:
but pull off first my bootes: make them cleane:
and then put my boot-hosen, and my
spurres therein: giue me my slippers.

Sirs, doth it please you to come to ⎰ *breakefast?*
dinner?
an vnchion?
supper?
drinking?

It is well said: for certainly I am verie hungrie

and thirstie: J am ⎰ *wearie.*

VVhere shall we dine? what folkes are
there within? do J not know them?

They be guests: come in, doth it please you
to dine with them? there is roome enough.

It is all one vnto vs: of whence are they?
of whence are you my friend? of what countrie

Marguerite, apportez icy un voirre, *verre*
une ſerviette et du pain: haſtez vous.
  Où avez vous eu ce vin? c'eſt le
meilleur que j'aye point bu de ſtannée. *ceſte annee*
  Je le ſuy allé querir loin d'icy: chez Monſ. N.
à la teſte du Roy, à Temple barre.
  Allez vous kerir voſtre vin ſi loin? *loing*
  Ouy, pour avoir du bon: car il y alà
couſtumiérement le meilleur vin de
Londres: et de toutes ſortes.
  Buvons en bien, tandiſ kil eſt bon:
maiſ tirez premier méſ bottes: nettoyez lés:
et puiſ mettez méſ tricoufes, et més
eſperonſ dedans: baillez més pantoufles. *eſperons*

Meſſieurs, vouſ plait-il venir
{
déjuner?
diſner?
gouſter? reciner?
ſouper?
faire colacion?
}

  C'eſt bien dit: car certeſ j'ay grand fain *faim*
et ſoif: je ſuy
{
las,
laſſé,
recreu,
tout haraſſé.
}
  Où diſneronſ nous? quel gens y a-il
là dedans? ne léſ cognoiſ-je point?
  Ce ſont hoſtes: entrez, vouſ plait-il
diſner avec eux? il y a placé aſſez.
  Ce nous eſt tout vn: d'où ſont-ilz?
d'où eſteſ vous mon amy? de kel païs

are you? Sir, let it not diſpleaſe you
if I aske your name? tell me your
name: what is your name? ſhall I be ſo bold
as to demaund your name? it ſhall not diſ-
pleaſe you, if I aske your name: how do
you call your name? how do they
call you? how ſhall I call you?
tell vs your name.

My name is Henrie Page: J am called
Humfrey Hoſe: I am of London:

I am { *a Frenchman,*   *an Italian,*
     an Engliſhman,   *an Almane,*
     a Spaniard,   *an Iriſhman,*
     a Scottiſhman,   *a Flemming.*

From vvhence come you now?

I come from { *France.*
     England.
     Turkie.
     Venice.

VVhither go you now?

I go to { *England.*
     Italie.
     Hungarie.
     Poland.

VVhat newes in Flanders?
vvhat newes haue they in Spaine?

vvhat ſay you of { *newes?*
     good?
     this?
     that?

eſteʒ vous? Monſieur, ne vouʒ déplaize   *desplaiſe*
ſi je demande voſtre non? diteʒ moy voſtre
non: quel eſt voſtre non? ſeray-je ſi hardi   *nom*
de demander voſtre non: il ne vouʒ déplai-
ra pas, ſi je demande voſtre non: commenʒ   *nom*
vous appelleʒ vous? commenʒ vous ap-
pelle on? commenʒ vous appelleray-je?
diteʒ nouʒ voſtre non.   *nom*

     Mon non eſt Henry Page: je m'appelle
Honfrey Has: je ſuiʒ de Londres:

Je ſuy $\left\{\begin{array}{ll} \text{François,} & \text{Italien,} \\ \text{Anglois,} & \text{Aleman,} \\ \text{Eſpagnol,} & \text{Irlandois,} \\ \text{Eſcoſſois,} & \text{Flaman.} \end{array}\right.$

     D'où veneʒ vouʒ maintenant?

Je vienʒ $\left\{\begin{array}{l} \text{de France.} \\ \text{d'Angleterre.} \\ \text{de Turkíe.} \\ \text{de Veniſe.} \end{array}\right.$

     Où alleʒ vous à ceſte ḫeure?

Je vay en $\left\{\begin{array}{l} \text{Angleterre.} \\ \text{Italie.} \\ \text{Hungríe.} \\ \text{Pologne.} \end{array}\right.$

     Quelleʒ nouvelles en Flandres?
que dit-on de nouvʒau en Eſpagne?

que diteʒ vouʒ de $\left\{\begin{array}{l} \text{nouvʒau?} \\ \text{bon?} \\ \text{cecy?} \\ \text{cela?} \end{array}\right.$

vvhat newes heare you? how goeth all
in this citie? are victuals good cheape here?
are victuals deare in France?

Surelie I know nothing of $\begin{cases} newes, \\ good, \\ but\ good: \end{cases}$

all goeth vvell: great cheare he that hath monie:
I heare no newes: no newes.

Sir, I thinke that I haue seene you sometime,
but I remember not where:
me thinketh to be at Lions.

You say true, I am of that place.

How $\begin{cases} do\ you? \\ goeth\ it\ with\ you? \\ is\ it\ with\ you? \end{cases}$

VVell $\begin{cases} at\ your\ commandement: \\ I\ thanke\ you: \\ God\ be\ thanked:\ I\ do\ well: \end{cases}$

at your commandement and seruice:

readie to do you $\begin{cases} pleasure: \\ seruice. \end{cases}$

How doth your health?
As you see: as I was wont:
so, so.

How do you in your businesse?
As I may, and not as J will.

Sirs, will it please you to $\begin{cases} wash? \\ sit? \\ sit\ at\ the\ table? \end{cases}$

It is well said mine host: where is

qu'oyez vous de nouveau, comment va tout
en ſte ville? fait-il bon vivre icy?
lẽs vivres ſont ilz chẽrs en France?

Certes je ne ſçay rien {
de nouveau:
de bon:
que bon:
}

tout va bien: grand chère ki a de l'argent: *qui*
je n'oy rien de nouveau: nulles nouvelles.

Monſ. je penſe que je vous ay veu d'autres fois,
mais je ne me ſouviens pas où:
il me ſemble que c'eſt à Lyon.

Vous dites vray, je ſuy de là.

Comment vous {
portez vous?
va?
eſt-il?
}

Bien, {
à voſtre commandement:
je vous remercíe:
Dieu mercy: je me porte bien
}

à voſtre commandement et ſervice:

preſt à vous faire {
plaiſir:
ſervice.
}

Comment ſe porte la ſanté?

Comme vous voyez: comme elle ſouloit:
tellement quellement.

Comment faites vous?

Meſſieurs, vous plait-il {
laver?
ſeoir?
mettre à table?
}

C'eſt bien dit mon hoſte: où eſt *dit*

mine hoſteſſe? cauſe her to come.

She will come anone: what wine
will it pleaſe you to drinke? ſpare not

the wine: for you are { *drie,*
hungrie,
hote,
cold.

make good cheare, and be merrie.

You ſay vvell, for it is { *hote:*
cold:
faire vveather:
foule vveather:
light.

Miſtreſſe, vvill it pleaſe you to giue me leaue
to drinke vnto you? Gentlevvoman, I
drinke to your good grace: I drinke to you.

Ʒ thanke you Sir: I thanke you
vvith all my heart: I vvill pledge you.

Giue me ſome { *browne*
vvheaten
vvhite
houſhold } *bread.*
ſtale
nevv
Sir, } *ſpice*
Miſtreſſe, } *of the houſe, I pray you let vs haue*
a quart of the beſt vvine that you haue.

VVith a good will Sir: me thinketh that you
know verie vvell our pots and meaſures,
although you be a ſtranger.

mon hoſteſſe? faiteʒ la venir.

Elle viendra incontinent: quel vin
vouʒ plait-il boire? n'eſpargneʒ paʒ

le vin: car vous aveʒ { ſoif:
faim:
chaud:
froid:

faim
chauld

faiteʒ bonne chère, eʒ rejouïſſeʒvous,

Vouʒ diteʒ bien, car il faiʒ { chaud:
froid:
beau tans:
laid.
clair.

Madame, vouʒ plait-il me donner congé
de boirę à vous? Madmoiſelle, je
boy à voſtre bonne grace: je boy à vous.

Madamoy-
ſelle

Grand mercy Monſieur: je vouʒ remercíe
de bien bon cœur: je vouʒ plègeré.

pledgeray

Donneʒ moy du pain { brun.
bis.
blanc.
de meſnage.
raſſis.
frais.
d'épice.

Monſieur ⎫
Madame ⎭ de ceans, je vouʒ prię ayons
une quarte du mejlleur vin que vous ayez.

Volontierʒ Monſieur, il me ſemble que vouʒ
coǧnoiſſeʒ forʒ bien noʒ potʒ eʒ meſures,
encor que ſoyez eſtranger.

Yea, but I knovv not your monie:
I praie you teach it me:
   Yes forsooth: I vvill teach you both:
the pint of Paris, is almoſt as great
as the quart of London: the quart, as the
pottle of England: the broc, or lot, as your
gallon: the ſeſtier, as your pint: the halfe
ſeſtier, as your penie pot: keepe that
well, for there is a ſmall difference.
   Hearken if I ſhall name them well:
halfe a ſeſtier, a ſeſtier, one pint,
one quart, a brocke, three quarts.
   Now let vs come to the monie:
a denier, a double, a liard, a blanke,
a ſizin, or halfe a ſous: a carolu, or
a granblanke: theſe kinds of monie be
vnder a ſhilling, which is worth twelue
pence: there be ſixtie ſous to the crowne
of the ſunne: foure teſters make a crowne.
   Tell me the value of euery peece.
   The denier of France, is worth halfe a
farthing of England: the double, a farthing:
the liard, a farthing and a halfe: foure pence,
or two doubles, the halfe penie of England:
the blanke, halfe penie and halfe farthing:
the ſizin, three farthings: the penie of En-
gland, maketh eight pence of France:
the carolu, otherwiſe called granblanke,
a penie farthing: the ſous, three halfe pence.
   VVhat ſay you of teſters, and halfe teſters?

Voire, mais je ne cognois pas voſtre monnoye: je vous prie enſeignez la moy.

Ouy dea: je vous enſeigneray lès deux:
la pinte de Paris, eſt preſque auſſi grande
que la quarte de Londres: la quarte, comme la
potelle d'Angl. le broc, ou le lot, comme voſtre
gallon: le ſeſtier, comme voſtre pinte: le demy
ſeſtier, comme voſtre peny pot: retenez bien
cela, car il y a peu de difference.

Eſcoutez ſi je lès nommeray bien:
un demy ſeſtier, un ſeſtier, une pinte,
une quarte, un broc, trois quartes.

Venons maintenant à la monnoye:
un denier, un double, un liard, un blanc,
un ſizain, ou un demy ſol: un carolu, ou
un grand blanc: toutes cès eſpèces ſont
au deſſoubz d'un ſol, lequel vaut douze
deniers: il y a ſoiſſante ſolz à l'eſcu
au ſoleil: quatre teſtons font l'eſcu.

Dites moy la valeur de chacune piéce.

Le denier de France, vaut un demy
fardin d'Angleterre: le double, un fardin:
le liard, un fardin et demy: quatre deniers,
ou deux doubles, la maille d'Angleterre:
le blanc, maille et demy fardin:
le ſizain, trois fardins: le denier d'Angleterre, fait huict deniers de France:
le carolu, autrement appelé grand blanc,
un denier fardin: le ſol, trois mailles.

Que dites vous dès teſtons, et demy teſtons?

ſixain

ſoixante

chaſcune

ſixain
faict huict

what call you peeces of three blankes,
and of ſixe blankes? I vnderſtand not their value.
 The teſter is worth eight pence of En-
gland: a peece of ſixe blankes, a groate.
 You miſreckon: at your reckning, the crowne
of the ſunne ſhould be more worth then
ſeuen ſhillings of England: furthermore,
they haue raiſed the monie.
 I put the matter to the merchants.
 Go to, let vs reckon my hoſt, that I
paie, and may be gone: vvhat owe J?
vvhat ovve vve? change me a
crovvne of gold, for I haue no ſingle monie.
 Is it of vveight? I cannot tell, vveigh it.

Of the weight.

PEter, *vvhere art thou? bring me the vveights:*
this crovvne is not vveight.
 VVeigh this Angell a little: the ballance
is not ſtraight: your hand ſhaketh.
 VVhat ſhall I vveigh, vvhen
it is not currant? it is too ſhort: it is of
baſe gold: it is light: it is clipped: it is
counterfeit: it is cleft: it is cracked: it is
not of good alley: it is not of good gold:
it is not of good ſiluer: it is called in:
it is too light of three graines: it is ſoudred:
J vvill none of it: change it me.
 J haue not coined it: giue me the reſt:

qu'appellez vouȿ piéceȿ de troiȿ blançs,
eṭ de fiȥ blançs? je n'entenȿ paȿ leur valeur.

Un teſton, vauṭ dix⁓ḫuiṭ denierȿ d'Angleterre: un piéce de fiȥ blançs, un gros.

Vouȿ vouȿ meſcontez: à voſtre conte l'eſcu   *compte*
fol̗ vaudroiṭ pluȿ de
ſepṭ chelinȿ d'Angleterre: d'avantage,
lon a rehauſſé la monnoyȩ.

Je m'en rapportȩ auȥ marchanṭs.

Or bien, contonȿ mon ḫoſte, que je   *comptons*
paye, eṭ que je m'en ail̗le: que doiḃȿ-je?
combien deḫvonȿ nous? changeȥ moy un
eſcu d'or, car je n'ay poinṭ de monnoyȩ.

Eſ̗t-il de poiḋȿ? Je ne ſcé, pezeȥ-le.   *ſçay*

Du Poids.

Pierre, où eȿ-tu? apporte-moy le poiḋȿ:
ſte cu n'eſſt paȿ de poiḋȿ.   *ceſt eſcu*

Pefez un peu ſtAngelot: la balance
n'eſſt paȿ droite: la ma̧in vouȿ tremble.

Que peſeray-je, quand
il n'eſſt paȿ de mize? il eſṭ tro̅p̅ court: il eſṭ   *miſe*
de bas or: il eſſt leger: il eſſt rongné: il eſṭ
faul̗x: il eſṭ fendu: il eſſt caſſé: il n'eſſt
paȿ de bon alloy: il n'eſſt paȿ de bon or:
il n'eſſt paȿ de bon argent: il eſṭ deſcrié:
il eſṭ courṭ de troiȿ gra̧ins: il eſſt ſoudé:
ie n'en veuȥ point: changeȥ-le moè.   *moy*

Je ne l'é paȿ cogné: donneȥ moy le reſte: *coigné*

my ſhe friend, call vnto me the horſe keeper:
my friend, ſaddle and bridle my horſe:
knit vp his taile: haue you dreſſed him vvell,
curried, rubbed, combed his maine?
looke if he be vvell ſhod: he lacketh
a naile, or two: where is the Smith?

   Here I am Sir, what ſhall I do?

   Shoo my horſe, and take
heed you pricke him not: me thinketh
that he halteth: how came that to paſſe?
horſe-keeper, hold there is to drinke: where
is the maiden? hold, my ſhe friend,
behold to buy pins, to the end that you
remember me another time.

   I thanke you Sir: ſpare not the
lodging, for it is at your commandement.

Farewell { *my hoſt: my hoſteſſe:*
all the companie:
till we ſee againe:
till I come againe.

   God be with you Sir: God be your keeper:

God { *keepe you from euill:*
guide you:
haue you in his keeping:
giue you a good and a long life:
giue you the accompliſhment
  of all your good deſires.

m'amye, appellez moy le vallet d'eſtable:
mon amy, ſelez et bridez mon cheval: *ſellez*
trouſſez ſa queuë: l'avez vous bien panſé,
eſtrillé, frotté, pigné lês crins?
regardez s'il eſt bien ferré: il luy faut
un clou ou deux: où eſt le mareſchal?

   Me voi-cy Monſieur, que feré-je?   *feray-je*

   Ferrez mon cheval, et donnez vous
garde de l'enclouër: il me ſemble
qu'il cloche, d'où vient cela?
palefrenier, tien, voila ton vin: où eſt
la chambriére? tenez m'amye,   *chambriere*
voila pour voz eſpingles, afin que vous
vous ſouvienez de moy une autre fois.   *aultre*

   Grand mercy Monſieur, n'eſpargnez pas
le logis, car il eſt à voſtre commandement.

          ⎧ mon hoſte: mon hoſteſſe:
Adieu ⎨ toute la compagnie:
          ⎪ juskes au revoir:
          ⎩ juskes au retour.   *uſques*

   Adieu Monſieur, Dieu ſoit garde de vous:

          ⎧ gard de mal:
          ⎪ conduiſe:
Dieu vous ⎨ ait en ſa garde:
          ⎪ doint bonne vie et longue:
          ⎪ doint l'accompliſſement
          ⎩   de tous voz bons deſirs.

Rules for Merchants, to buy
and fell.

Landi, is a
faire in Paris,
fo called.

S^{Ir}, *whither ride you fo foftly?*
    To London, to Bartholomew faire:
I go to Landi, to Paris: I go to Roan.
    And I alfo: let vs go together: J am
verie glad to haue found companie.

Let vs go ⎰ *in Gods name:*
          ⎱ *in a good houre:*
          ⎰ *vvith a good lucke:*
let vs pricke a little: let vs make haft:
J feare vve fhall not come thither
by daie light, for the funne goeth downe.

    But vvhere fhall vve lodge? vvhere is the
beft lodging? the beft Inne?

    Care you not for that: it is
at the great market, at the figne of the
flovver-deluce, right ouer againft the croffe.

    I am glad that I am arriued, for
trulie I haue a good ftomacke: I hope to
make to night a merchants fupper.

    VVe faie in our countrie, that hunters
breakefaft, lavvyers dinner, fupper
of merchants, and Monkes drinking,
is the beft cheare that one can make,
and liue like an Epicure.

    And they fay in our Parifh, that yong

Pour Merchands, acheter
& vendre.

MOnſieur, où pikeȥ vous ſi bellement?   *cheuauchez*
  A Londres, à la foire de la Barthelemy:
je vay au Landi, à Paris: je vay à Roan.

  Et moy auſſi: allons enſemble: je ſuy
bien aiſe d'avoir trouvé compagnie.

Allons ⎰ de par Dieu:
      ⎱ au nom de Dieu:
      { à la bonne heure:
      ⎰ à la bonne adventure:
piquons un peu: haſtons nous:
j'ay peur que nous ne venions pas là
de jour, car le ſoleil s'en va coucher.

  Mais où logerons nous? où eſt le
meilleur logis? la meilleure hoſtelerie?

  Ne vous ſouciez pas de cela: *ſoulciez*
c'eſt au grand marché, à l'enſeigne de la
fleur de Lis, vis à vis de la croix.

  Je ſuy joyeux d'eſtre arrivé, car
certes j'ay bon appetit: j'eſpère de
faire à ce ſoir ſouper de marchant.

  Nous diſons en noſtre païs, que deſju-
ner de chaſſeurs, diſner d'advocats, ſouper
de marchants, et collacion de Moynes,
eſt la meilleure chère qu'on ſauroit faire:
et pour vivre en Epicurien.

  Et on dit en noſtre paroiſſe que jeunes

Phiſitions make the Church-yards crooked;
and old Atturneys ſutes to go avvrie: but
on the contrarie, yong Atturneys and
old Phiſitions, yong fleſh and old
fiſh be the beſt.

But being vpon talking of Phiſitions,
how cometh that the good do neuer
or ſeldome take anie Phiſicke?

But where haue you ſeene a good Counſeller
in law, to pleade for himſelfe?

You ſay true: what is the cauſe?

The reaſon is, that they be wiſe and circumſpect.

VVell, ſhall we go and buy that which
we do lacke? we tarrie too long.

Rowland, why doeſt thou not riſe? open
the ſhop: art thou yet in bed?
thou loueſt the feathers well: if my
maiſter cometh downe, and find not
the ſhop opened, he will be angrie.

Sirs, Sir, my Ladie, miſtris, gentlewoman,
what lacke you? what ſeeke you?
what would you buy willingly?
what will it pleaſe you to buy? aske
you anie thing? ſee if I haue
anie thing which liketh you: J will
make you good cheape: one will make you
as good cheape as in anie ſhop in
this towne: as in anie ſhop in
London: enter in: behold, the ſight
ſhall coſt you nothing: you ſhall reſt:

médecins font lès cymitiéres boſſus:
eṭ veux procureurs procès tortus: mais
au contraire, que jeuneṣ procureurs, eṭ
vieux médecins, jeune chaire, eṭ
vieịl poiſſon font lèṣ meịlleurs.

    Mais à propoṣ dèṣ médecins,
d'où vienṭ que lèṣ bons ne prenneṇṭ
jamais, ou rarement, médecine?

    Mais où aveẓ vouṣ vẹu un bon aḍvocat
aḍvocaſſer eṭ plaider pour ſoy-meſme?

    Vouṣ diteṣ vray: kellẹ en eṣṭ la cauſe?

    Pour ce qu'ilz fonṭ ſages, eṭ bien aḍviſez.

    Or bien, ironṣ nous acheter ce qu'il
nouṣ faut, nouṣ demouronṣ trop.

    Roland, que ne te leveṣ tu? ouvre
la boutique: eṣ tu encorẹ au lit?   *liā*
tu aimeṣ bien la plume: ſi mon
maiṣtre deſcenḍ, eṭ qu'il ne trouve
la boutiquẹ ouverte, il ſe courroucera.

    Meſſieurs, Monſieur, madame, madamoiſelle,
que demandeẓ vous? que cercheẓ vous?
qu'acheterieẓ vouṣ volontiers?
que vouṣ plait-il acheter? demandeẓ
vouṣ quelque choſe? regardeẓ ſi j'ay
quelque choſe qui vouṣ duiſe: je vouṣ
feray bon marché: lon vouṣ fera
auſſi bon marché qu'en boutique de
ceṣte ville: qu'en boutique qui ſoiṭ danṣ
Londres: entrez: voyez, la veuë ne
vouṣ couṣtera rien: vouṣ vouṣ repoſerez:

you shall chuse   } for your monie.
you shall haue the choise }

   You haue no velvet, cloth,
sattin of such colour as I do
lacke: kerseis Flanders dying:
blacke, vvhite, yellow, violet, changeable,
tawnie, browne, red, skie colour, scarlet, blue,
migren, greene, murrie, graie,
orange, vnwatered chamlet, vvatered,
damaske, vvofted, buckram, farfnet, millan
fuftian, cloth of gold, of filuer, and cypres?

   Sir, come in: I haue all
forts of filke, cloth of all colours,
of all prifes, at choice, and good cheape.

   Vnfold this peece of crimfon velvet:
for how much fell you an ell?
vvhat shall I giue you for a yard?
vvhat shall I paie for the vvhole peece?
do not ouerprife it:

let vs haue but { one vvord: make short.

   VVill you but a vvord? twentie shillings
an ell: the yard vvill coft you xix shillings
and halfe: is it not faire?

   I haue feene fairer, better and
vvorfe also: it is too much: it is too deare:
you ouerfell your { vvare:
                  { marchandife:
you are too deare.

   Sir, vvhat vvill you giue for it? that I

vous choifirez ⎫
vous aurez le chois ⎬ pour voftre argent.
      ⎭

  Vous n'avez point de veloux, de drap,
de fatin de telle couleur que j'en
demande: dès crefeaux teinture de Flanders:
de noir, de blanc, jaune, violet, changeant,
tanné, brun, rouge, pers, efcarlate, bleu,
couleur de migraine, verd, morée, gris,
orange, camelot fans onde, ondoyé:
damas, oftade, bougran, taffetas, fuftaine
de millan, drap d'or, drap d'argent, et crefpe?

  Monfieur, entrez dedans: j'ay toutes fortes
de drap de foye, de toutes couleurs,
de tous priz, à choifir, et à bon marché.

  Defployez fte piéce de veloux cramoifi:
combien vendez vous l'aune?
ke donneray-je de la verge?
ke payeray-je de la piéce entiére?
ne le me furfaites pas:

n'ayons ⎰ qu'une parolle:
   ⎱ qu'un mot: faites le court.

  Ne voulez vous qu'un mot: vingt folz
l'aune: la verge vous couftera dixneuf folz
et demy: n'eft-il pas beau?

  J'en é veu de plus beau, de meilleur et   *ay*
de pire auffi: c'eft trop: c'eft trop chèr:

vous furfaites voftre ⎰ danrée:
        ⎱ marchandife:
vous eftes trop chèr.

  Monfieur, qu'en baillerez vous? à fin ke je

may fell: I hope that you bring me
good lucke: looke on it at your leifure:
it is of a faire breadth: it is verie broad:
it hath an ell of breadth: fhall J meafure it?

    How make you the whole peece?

    You fhall giue xxv. pounds
fifteene f. it is but xviij f.
fixe pence halfe penie the yard.

    Haue you none better?

    I will fhew you the faireft
and beft in London, yea that euer you
did handle: but it is deare.

    I care not whatfoeuer it coft,
if it be faire and good.

    Behold Sir: did you euer fee
better, and fairer colour?

    Vnfold it: vnfold it not all:
fold it now, J haue had
the fight thereof: how manie elles be in it?
it is verie narrow, as me thinketh.

    There be xxv. elles and a halfe,
and halfe a quarter, and good meafure.

    You will make me beleeue it.

    Truly that prentice hath a good tongue:
he waiteth for his mafters profit.

    Doth he not well? it is his trade:
well, fhall I haue it at that price?

    At what price Sir? you know
what I haue told you: J am a man of one
word: I cannot fell it for leffe,

vende: j'efpére ke vouʒ m'apportez
bon ḫeur: regardez le à voſtrę aiſe:
il eſt de belle largeur: il eſt bien large:
il a unę aune de large: le meſureray-je?

    Combien faiteʒ vouʒ la piécę entiére?

    Vous en baịllerez vin͠gt eṭ cin͠͠q livreʒ
quinze foḷz: ce n'eſt que dix-ḫuiçṭ foḷz
fiͯx deniers eṭ maịlle la verge.

    N'en aveʒ vouʒ poinṭ de meịlleur?

    Je vous en monſtreray le pluʒ bęau
eṭ meịlleur de Londres, voire que vouʒ
maniaſteʒ jamais: mais il eſt chêr.

    Il ne m'en chauṭ quoy qu'il couſte,   *chault*
pour-veu qu'il foiṭ bęau eṭ bon.

    Regardez Monſieur, en vęiſteʒ vouʒ jamaiʒ
de meịlleur, eṭ pluʒ belle couleur?

    Deſployez-le: ne le deſployez paʒ tout:
repliez-le mạintenant, j'en ay eu
la veuë: combien y en a-il d'aunes?
il eſt fort eſtroit, ce me femble.   *eſtroict*

    Il y en a vin͠gt cinq aunes eṭ demye,
eṭ un demy quartier, à bonne mefure.   *vng*

    Vouʒ le me voulez fairę à croire.

    Certeʒ ceſt apprentif a bonne langue:
il veille pour le profiṭ de fon maiſtre.

    Ne fait-il paʒ bien? c'eſt fon meſtier:
or bien, l'auray-je à ce prix?

    A quel priͯx Monſieur? vous fçavez ce
que je vous ay dit: je fuis ḫome d'une
parolle: je ne le fauroyę vendrę à moins,   *fçaurois*

except *J* would lofe in it: and truly you
feeke not my loffe, as *J* thinke.

    You make your ware out of
reafon: fo we will go fomewhere elfe,
for your price is not for vs.

    As it fhall pleafe you: go where it
will feeme good vnto you: neuertheleffe, I
may affure you of one thing, that when
you fhould go by all the fhops and
warehoufes of London, you cannot
find the like offer as I make vnto you:
notwithftanding if you find not better,
come againe, you know my price:
indeed I make you better cheape
by a groate in a yeard, becaufe that
I hope to fell to you fome of my merchandize:
becaufe you are my cuftomer:
becaufe you are accuftomed
to buy your prouifion here within:

J will bate you a $\begin{cases} penie, \\ groate, \\ fhilling, \\ crowne\ vpon\ the\ peece, \end{cases}$

to the end that I may haue $\begin{cases} your\ hanfell: \\ of\ your\ money. \end{cases}$

    VVe cannot agree, as I perceiue:
let vs go to fee the faire.

    Let vs go $\begin{cases} where\ it\ will\ pleafe\ you: \\ where\ you\ will: \\ when\ you\ will: \end{cases}$

ſi je n'y vouloyę perdre: eţ certeş vouş
ne cercheʒ paş ma perte, comme je penſe.

Vouş faiteş voſtre danrée horş de
raiſon, par ąinſi nous irons ąjlleurs,
car voſtre priʒ n'eſt paş pour nous.

Commę il vouş plaira: allez où
bon vous ſemblera: touteş‿fois, je
vouş peux aſſeurer d'une choſe, que quanḑ
vous irieʒ par touteş lės boutiques eţ
magaſinş de Londres, vouş ne ſaurieʒ
trouver vn tel offre que je vouş ſay:
non‿obſtanţ ſi vouş ne trouveʒ mieux,
revenez, vous ſçaveʒ mon prix:
en verité je vouş ſay mejlleur marché
d'un groʒ pour verge, à cauſe que
j'eſpère vouş vendre de ma marchandiſe:
pource que vous eſteş mon chalant:
à cauſe que vous avez accouſtumé
d'acheter voſtre fourniture ceans:

je vouş rabbatray un $\left\{\begin{array}{l}\text{denier,}\\ \text{gros,}\\ \text{ſol,}\\ \text{eſcu ſur la piece,}\end{array}\right.$

afin que j'ayę $\left\{\begin{array}{l}\text{voſtrę eſtrène:}\\ \text{de voſtrę argent.}\end{array}\right.$

Nouş ne nouş pouvons accorder, comme
je voy: allonş vęoir la foire.

Allons $\left\{\begin{array}{l}\text{où il vouş plaira:}\\ \text{où vouş voudrez:}\\ \text{quanḑ vouş voudrez:}\end{array}\right.$

ſçauriez
fais
mieulx

let vs walke through the faire.

J am content: there ſhall be no let by me.

VVilliam, where be thoſe merchants
which I haue left here in the ſhop?
haue they bought anie thing?

They be gone: they haue bought nothing.

Call them againe, for it is readie monie.

They are entred into another ſhop:
I ſee them which come againe.

They ſhall be welcome if they bring
monie: if it be ſo that they bring.

You make vs trauell much: J
pray you diſpatch vs all at once:

cauſe vs not to { *tarrrie ſo long:*

go and come ſo much:
we be in haſt: we are farre off.

Jt is not my fault: I deſire nothing
but to ſell: I ſeeke but monie.

Shall we haue the whole peece for
nine pounds? as much at one word,
as at an hundred: at the laſt word.

Truly you be importunate: you care
not whether I loſe or gaine: you
ſhall not bate a halfe penie of ten
pounds? when you ſhould buy
all that is in the ſhop: and trulie
if you leaue it, no man in the world
ſhall haue it for the price: if it

allonʃ nouʃ pourmener par~my la foire.

J'en ʃuy content: il ne tiendra pas à moy.

Guillaume, où ʃonʇ cêʃ marchanʇʃ
que jé laiʃʃé icy en la boutique?
ont-ilz acheté quelque choʃe?

Ilz s'en ʃont allez: ilʐ n'onʇ rien acheté.

Rappeleʐ les, car ceʃt argenʇ contant.

Ilz ʃont entrez en unę autre boutique:
je lêʃ voy qui reviennenʇ.

Ilz ʃeronʇ lêʃ bien venus s'ilz apportenʇ
argent: pourvęu qu'ilz apportenʇ.

Vouʃ nouʃ faiteʃ bęaucouƀ travaįller: je
vouʃ príe dépeʃcheʐ nouʃ touʇ d'une traite:

ne nouʃ faiteʃ pluʃ tanʇ {
  demourer:
  tarder:
  attendre:
  aller eʇ venir:
}

nous avonʃ haʃte: nous ʃommeʃ de loin.

Ce n'eʃt paʃ ma faute: je ne demande
qu'à vendre: je ne cerche quę argent.

faulte

Auronʃ nouʃ la piécę entiére pour
neuf livres? autant en un mot,
qu'en un cent: tout au dernier mot.

Certeʃ vous eʃtes importuns: il ne
vous chaut, ʃi je pers ou gagne: vouʃ
n'en rabbatreʐ pas une maįlle de diʐ
livres, quanđ vous acheterieʐ
touʇ ce qui eʃt en la boutique: eʇ certes
ʃi vouʃ le laiʃʃez, perʃonne du monde
ne l'aura pour le prix, quanđ ce ʃeroiʇ

were my brother: I bate you xx. ſ.
becauſe I will not let you go:
if I might leaue it for a leſſer price,
you ſhould haue it as ſoone as
any man in the world, chiefly for
acquaintance ſake.

 VVell, J truſt you, tell money:

haue we not here { *a porter?*

come hither, lay that vpon thy backe, and
carrie it to my lodging, at the three Kings in
Fleetſtreet, and tell mine hoſt that they prepare
the ſupper, for we will come by and by.

 Truly here is faire paiment.

 Pay your ſelfe in gold or in ſiluer:
chuſe: J giue you the choiſe.

 It is all one vnto me, the money is as
good vnto me as gold: I would that

he which hath coined { *this ſhilling*

had his eares nailed to the pillorie:
to the poſt of the doore: had his eares cut off:
to the end that all falſe coiners of money
might take example thereby: what ſay you to it?

 I would, and that it had coſt me
a quart of wine: Farewell, haue me
commended: are you content?

 Yea Sir, I thanke you: ſpare

mon frère: je vouſ rabbatſ vinſt ſoſz,
à cauſe que je ne vouſ veuſ pas eſconduire:
ſi je le pouvoyſ laiſſer à moindre prix,
vouſ l'auriez auſſi toſt kome   *que homme*
du monde, meſmemenſ pour
l'amour de coſnoiſſance.

    Or bien, je me fiſ en vous: comptez argent:

n'avonſ nouſ point icy de $\begin{cases}\text{crocheteur?}\\\text{porte-faix?}\\\text{fakin?}\end{cases}$

viens-çà, charge cela ſur ton doz, eſ le
portſ en mon logis, au troiſ Rois en
Flitſtrit: eſ di à mon hoſte kon appreſte   *qu'on*
le ſouper, car nouſ viendrons incontinent.

    Certeſ voi-cy bſau payement.

    Payeſ vous en or, ou en argent:
choiſiſſez: je vous en baſlle le choix.

    Ce m'eſt tout un: la monnoyſ m'eſt
auſſi bonne que l'or: je vouſdroyſ que

celuy qui a $\left.\begin{array}{l}\text{forgé,}\\\text{coigné,}\\\text{batu}\end{array}\right\}$ ce ſou,   *ſol*

ſuſt lèſ oreilleſ clouées au pilori:
au poſteau de l'huis: fuſt eſſorillé:
afin que touſ lèſ faulſ-monnoyeurs
y prinſeſt exemple: qu'en diteſ vous?

    Je le vouſdroyſ, eſ qu'il m'euſt couſté   *voudrois*
une quarte de vin: Adieu, je me
recommande: eſteſ vouſ contant?   *content*

    Ouy Monſieur, je vouſ remercſe: n'eſpargnez

nothing that I haue, as well without monie,
as with monie: J will giue you
credit for three moneths: J will
trust you a yeare, yea two,

vpon your { *word,*
promise,
obligation,
bill of your hand:

in putting { *suretie.*

J thanke you Sir: I will not forsake you
for another: trulie that merchant is honest:
I cannot tell whether he would do as he saith.

{ *Let vs proue it.*

Jt shall be for another time: let vs
buy some babies for our children:
shall we? it is well said.

Proverbes.

Aister Claudius, I praie you
teach me how I may

rule my selfe to { *applie*

certaine French Prouerbes with

chofe que j'ayę, auffi bien fans argent,
qu'avec argent: je vouş bailleray
à credit pour troiş moys: je vouş
feray credit pour un an, voire deux,

fur voftre {
parolle,
promeffe,
obligacion,
cédule:
}

me donnant {
plège,
caucion,
affeurance.
}

Grand mercy Sire: je ne vouş lairray paş   *laiſſeray*
pour un autre: certes ce marchant eſt ḥoneſte:
ie ne fçay s'il feroit ce qu'il dit.

Efprouvonş- }
Effayonş- } le.

Ce fera unę autre fois: achetonş dèş   *acheptons*
poupetteş pour noz enfantş:
feronş nous? Ceſt bien dit.

Proverbes.

MAiſtre Claude, ie vouş prię
enfegnez moy comment ie me   *enſeignez*

doy governer pour {
approprier,
adapter,
appliquer,
accommoder,
apparier
}
    doibt

certainş Proverbeş François avec

the Englifh, and you fhall do me a pleafure.
  VVith all my heart: I haue here gathered
fome, which although they agree
not in all points touching the words,
notwithflanding in the meaning they agree
very well: as if you would
fignifie that one offereth you helpe too late,
or a thing whofe vfe is alreadie
paffed for the prefent: we fay
in French, after death, the Phifition:
and the Englifh faith, after dinner
muftard: neuerthele∬e the moft
part of thefe here gathered in this Pamphlet,
do anfwer one another both in words
and fence.

Let vs heare then which be thofe Prouerbes.

A *Carrion kite will neuer be*
  good hauke.
  He is as poore as Job.
  It is good to beate the iron while it is hote.
  He robbeth Peter, to pay
Paul.
  The burned child dreadeth the fire.
  A foft pace goeth farre.
  It is good to haue two ftrings to his bow.
  He that cometh laft, maketh
the doore faft.

l'Anglois, et vous me ferez plaifir.

De bien bon cœur: j'en ay icy recueilli
quelques uns, lefquelz encore qu'ilz ne
conviennent du tout quant aux parolles,
toutes-fois en fens ilz s'accordent
fort bien: comme fi vous vouliez
fignifier kon vous offre trop tard fecours,   *qu'on*
ou la chofe dont l'ufage en eft
paffé pour le prefent: nous difons
en François, après la mort, le médecin:
et l'Anglois dit, après difner de la
mouftarde: mais fi eft-ce que la plus
part de ceulx-cy ramaffez en ce livret,
s'entre-refpondent et en parolles,
et au fens.

Oyons donc qui font
ces Proverbes.

ON ne fauroit faire d'une bufe
un efprevier.

Il eft povre comme Job.

Il fait bon batre le fer, tandis qu'il eft chaud.

Il ofte à Saint Pierre, pour donner à
Saint Pol.   *Paul*

Chien efchaudé craint l'eaue froide.

Allez tout beau fans vous efchauffer.

Il fait bon avoir deux chordes en fon arc.

Le dernier ferme la porte, ou
la laiffe ouverte.

If the skie fall, we ſhall
haue larkes.

You are good to be a poore mans ſow.

Like maſter, like man.

One ſcabbed ſheepe will marre
the whole flocke.

He that hath a good neighbour,
hath a good morrow.

Hunger is the beſt ſauce.

Looke not a giuen horſe in
the mouth.

Sweete meate muſt haue ſowre ſauce.

Neare is my peticoate, but nearer is my ſmocke.

The nearer the Church, the further from God.

When the belly is full, the bones would haue reſt.

The cat loueth fiſh, but ſhe loueth not
to wet her paw.

She is as buſie as a hen with two
chickens.

Faire words hurt not the mouth.

Betwixt two ſtooles the arſe goeth downe.

It is euill halting before a creeple.

There is no fire without ſmoke.

VVhen the ſteed is ſtolen, then ſhut
the ſtable doore.

Better late thriue, then neuer.

Good wine needeth no buſh.

The pot goeth ſo often to the water, that at
the laſt it cometh broken home.

Si le ciel tomboit, lês cailles
feroyent prinzes.

prinſes

    Il feroit bonne truye à povre home.

    Quel maiſtre, tel vallet.

    Il ne faut qu'une brebiş rongneuſe,
pour gaſter tout le troupeau.

    Qui a bon voiſin,
a bon matin.

    Il n'y a faulce que d'appetit.

    A cheval donné, il ne faut paş re-
garder aux dens.

    Pour un plaiſir, mille douleurs.

    Ma chemiſe m'eſt pluş prèş ke ma robe.

    Prèş de léglize, loin de Dieu.

l'egliſe

    De la pance, vient la danſe.

    Le chat aime le poiſſon, mais il
n'aime pas à mouiller la patte.

    Il eſt empefché comme une poule
qui n'a qu'un poulſin.

    Belleş parolleş n'eſcorchent paş la langue

    Il a le cul entre deux ſelles.

    Il ne faut paş clocher devant un boiteux.

    Nul feu ſanş fumée.

    Il eſt tanş de fermer l'eſtable, quand
lès chevaux s'en font allez.

    Il vaut mieux tard, que jamais.

    A bon vin, il ne faut point d'enſeigne.

    Tant ſouvent va le pot à l'eaue, que
l'anſe y demeure.

A friend in the Court
is worth a penie in the purſe.
   He that reckoneth without his hoſt,
muſt reckon twiſe.
   He hath put the fire to the tow.
   He ſetteth the cart before the horſes.
   A rolling ſtone gathereth
no moſſe.
   All is not gold that gliſtereth.
   Few words among wiſe men do ſuffice.
   He cutteth a large thong of another mans leather.
   He beareth fire in one hand, and
water in the other.
   To buy a pig in a poke.
   He beareth two faces vnder one hood.
   Loue me and loue my dog.
   All couet, all loſe.
   After a ſtorme cometh a calme.
   Better bow then breake.
   The king loſeth his right, where
nothing is to be had.
   Ft is a good horſe that neuer ſtumbleth.
   Saue a theefe from the gallowes,
and he will cut your throate.
   Rome was not built in one day.
   A fooles bolt ſoone ſhot.
   Firſt borne, firſt ſerued.

Bon fait avoir amy en cour,
car le procès en eſt pluſ court.

Qui compte ſans ſon hoſte,
il luy convient compter deux fois.

Il a miſ le feu aux eſtoupes.

La charruë va devant lèſ bœuſs.

La pierre ſouvent remuëe, n'amaſſe
paſ volontierſ moſſe.

Tout ce qui luit n'eſt pas or.

A bon entēdeur il ne faut que demyç parolle.

Il coupe large courroyç du cuir d'autrui.

Il porte le feu et
l'eauç.

Acheter chat en poche.

Il a une façç à deux viſages.

Qui aime Jan, aime ſon chien.   *Jehan*

Qui trop empoigne, rien n'eſtraind.

Aprèſ la pluye vient le bçau temps.

Il vaut mieux tirer, que rompre.

Le Roy perd ſa rente, où
il n'a que prendre.

Il n'y a ſi bon cheval, qui ne bronche.

Oſtez un vilain du gibet, il
vous y mettra.

Rome n'a eſté baſtíe toutç en un jour

De fol juge, brieve ſentence.

Qui premier naiſt, premier paiſt.

Golden ſayings.

YOu haue ſhewed me faire Prouerbes,
wherefore I thanke you: if you haue
ſome faire ſayings, let it pleaſe you
to make vs partakers thereof: for I know
that the French tongue is not without ſuch.

I will tell you ſome verie ſhort, but
full of ſence as may be poſſible: the firſt is,
In a Prince loyaltie.

VVould God that this were well
printed in the hearts of all magiſtrates.
It is well begun, follow.

In a Clerke humilitie.

Trulie it is as a Philoſopher ſaid,
the more a man is learned,
the more he ought to humble himſelfe.

In a Prelate wiſedome.

The ſame is according vnto the Scripture
which ſaith, Ye are the ſalt of the earth.

In a Knight manhood: valiantneſſe.

Adde thereunto wiſedome: for the
outward ſtrength doth profit little,
except it be gouerned by the mother
of all vertues, which is diſcretion.

In a rich man liberalitie.

But without making any reckoning
of vſurers, becauſe they are neither
dead nor aliue: and do neuer
good, except they be dead indeed.

Mots dorez.

VOus m'avez monſtré de joliş Proverbes,
   donţ je vouş remercíe: ſi vous avez
quelque bȩaux diȼtions, il vouş plaira
de nous en faire participanţs: car je ſcé   *ſçay*
que la langue Françoiſe n'en eſt paş deſtituée.

   Je vous en diray de forţ brefz, mais
ſententieus au poſſible: le premier ſera:
   En Prince loyaulté.
   Pleuſt à Dieu que cela fuſt bien
engravé au cœur de touş Magiſtraţs.
Ceſt bien commencé, pourſuivez.
   En Clerc ḥumilité.
   Certes c'eſt-ce que diſoit un Philoſophe,
tanţ pluş que l'ḥomȩ eſt doȼte,
eţ tanţ plus il ſe doiḃt ḥumilier.
   En Prelaţ ſapience.
   Cela eſt ſelon l'Eſcriṗture,
laquelle dit: Vous eſteş le ſel de la terre.
   En Chevalier prouëſſe.
   Adjouſtez y auſſi ſageſſe: car la
forcȩ extérieure profite peu,
ſi elle n'eſt gouvernée par la mère
de touteş vertus, qui eſt diſcrétion.
   En richȩ ḥome largeſſe.
   Mais c'eſt ſanş mettrȩ en conte lȇs
uſuriers: à cauſe qu'ilz ne ſonţ ne
mors ne vifz: eţ ne fonţ jamaiş
bien, s'ilz ne ſonţ morţs de fait.

Jn a learned man eloquence.
This is not found fulfilled
in all men of learning.
Jn a merchant faithkeeping.
You do except all the bankerouts.
Jn a seruant obedience.
It is a good treasure, of a good
seruant and a good wife:
but J pray you, how do you call
in Latin a good wife?
Find her to me first, and J will
tell it you: for according vnto the doctrine
of Plato, one cannot name a
thing, which cannot be found at all.
Ah, you haue stopped my mouth:
neuerthelesse I haue heard name a good vvife:
vvill you know how?
J pray do, and for a like turne.
Hearken vvell, and print it in
your mind.
A good vvife, a good mule, and a
good goate, be three euill beasts.
In a vvoman chastitie.
Indeed Plautus saith, that she vvhich is chast
bringeth with her a faire dowrie.
In vvine good smell.
This pleaseth me verie well.
VVhat, do you loue vvine so vvell?
I should not be a Frenchman, if I should not loue
wine: and indeed I loue the sight thereof

En home docte eloquence.

Ceſtuy-cy ne ſe trouve pas accompli
en touſ lèſ gentſ ſçavantſ.

En marchant foy tenir.

Vous en exceptez lèſ banque⌣routiers.

En ſervant obeïſſance.

C'eſt un grand threſor, que d'un bon
ſerviteur, et d'une bonne fame:
maiſ je vouſ prie, comment appelez vous
en Latin une bonne fame?   *femme*

Trouvez la moé premiérement, et je   *moy*
le vouſ diray: car ſelon la doctrine
de Plato, on ne peult nommer une
choſe, qui ne ſe trouve point.

Ah vouſ m'avez fermé la bouche:
touteſ⌣fois, j'ay ouï nommer une bonne fame:
voulez vous ſçavoir comment?

Je vous en prie, et pour la pareille.

Eſcoutez bien, et l'imprimez en
voſtre entendement.

Une bonne fame, une bonne mule, et une
bonne chevre, ſont troiſ meſchanteſ beſtes.

En fame continence.

De vray Plaute dit, que celle qui eſt chaſte,
apporte un beau douäire.

En vin bonne odeur.

Stuy-cy me plait fort bien.   *ceſtuy*

Comment, aimez vous ſi bien le vin?

Je ne ſeroye paſ François, ſi je n'aimoye le   *ſerois*
vin: et de fait, j'en aime bien la veuë,

verie well, but the taſt pleaſeth me better.

   In cloth good colour.

   I bought the other day ſome ſtamell,
which is alreadie all ſtained.

   In an Herauld knowledge.

   Me thinketh that ours is not
verie skilfull in his art, becauſe
that he hath not yet ſpecified

nor declared $\left\{ \right.$ *mine armes.*

   J am not an Herauld, but
I know well your armes.

   VVhich be they, I pray you?

   They be the foure fingers and the
thombe: are they not faire?

   Gods bodekin, thoſe be the armes of a villaine,
and I am a Gentleman: but me
thinketh that we go out of our purpoſe:
we leape to the tale of Robin Hood:

$\left\{ \right.$ *follow your talke.*

   Theſe which do follow be of
$\left\{ \right.$ *another ſtuffe.*

maiſ le gouſt me plaiṭ mieux.

   En drap̃ bonne couleur.

   J'achetay l'autre jour de l'eſtamel,
lequel eſt deſja touṭ détaint.   *deſtaint*

    En Herauld coñnoiſſance.

   Il me ſemble que le noſtre n'eſt
paſ fort expert en ſon art, acauſe qu'il
ne m'a pas encore ſpécifié

ny declaré { mès armes.
{ mès armoiries.
{ mon eſcuſſon.

   Je ne ſuy pas Herauld, maiſ
je coñnoy bien voz armoiries.

    Quelles ſont elleſ je vouſ prie?

    Ce ſonṭ lèſ quatre doiĝṭs eṭ le
poulce: ne ſont elleſ paſ belles?

     Vertu bieu, ce ſonṭ lès armeſ d'un vilain,
eṭ je ſuy gentil‿home: mais il me
ſemble que nous ſortons horſ de propoz:
nous ſautonſ du coq à l'aſne:
{ ſuivez voſtre pointe:
{ pourſuivez voſtre propoz.

    Ceux qui s'enſuiveṇt, ſonṭ
{ d'un autre calibre.
{ d'unę autrę étoffe.

Seuen things which the chaſte
Romaines did ſhun.

1 TO talke much in feaſts and aſſemblies.
2 To eate too much in bankets.
3 To drinke wine being in health.
4 To ſpeake aſide with other men.
5 To lift vp their eyes in the temple.
6 To ſtay long at their vvindowes.
7 To go out of their houſes vvithout their husbands.

God hateth ſix things, and the ſeuenth
he abhorreth aboue all.

1 AN outragious eye.
2 A falſe tongue.
3 The hands polluted with murther.
4 The heart counſelling and doing euill.
5 The feete readie to do euill.
6 Falſe vvitneſſes.
7 Thoſe vvhich ſow ſtrife among brethren.

Three things be faire before
God and men.

1 AGreement among brethren.
2 Loue among neighbours.
3 The man and his vvife keeping faith
   and loyaltie together.

Sept chofes dont les chaftes Ro-
maines fe gardoyent.

1 PArler bȩaucoup eȿ feſtes eṭ aſſemblées.
2   Troꝑ manger èȿ convives.
3 Boire du vin eſtans faines.
4 Parler à part avec lěȿ ḥomes.
5 Haulʃer lěȿ yeux auȼ temples.
6 Eſtre bȩaucouꝑ de temꝑs auȼ feneſtres.
7 Sortir horȿ la maifon fanȿ leurȿ maris.

Dieu haiſt fix chofes, & la feptiefme
il abhorre fur tout.

1 L'œil outrageus
2   Une faulʃe langue.
3 Lěȿ mȧinȿ poluëȿ de meurtre.
4 Le cœur confeiḷlant eṭ faifanṭ mal.
5 Lěȿ piedȿ preſṭz à faire mal.
6 Lěȿ fauȼ tefmoinǧȿ.
7 Ceulȼ qui fèmeṇṭ diſſencion entre lěȿ frères.

Trois chofes font belles devant
Dieu & les homes.

1 ACcord entre frères.
2   Amitié entre voifins.
3 L'ḥome eṭ fa fame gardanṭȿ foy
    eṭ loyauté enfemble.

Three things odious and tedious.

1   A Begger proud.
2   A rich man a lyer.
3   { An old man lecherous.

Foure things be hurtfull if one go about them too haftily.

1   A T the fight, or at the warre.
2   At gluttonie, or gaming.
3   To a banket, if one be not called to it.
4   To talke, or reafon with a foole.

No bodie ought to let thefe foure things.

1   H E which will lawfully marrie.
2   He which goeth to fchoole.
3   He which will helpe the needie.
4   He which of a wicked life
      returneth to vertue.

It is not good to truft fiue things.

1   V Nto a ftrange dog.
2   Vnto an hired horfe.
3   Vnto a pratling woman.

Trois choſes odieuſes et faſcheuſes.

1 VN mandiant orguilleux.
2 Vn richę ħome menteur.
3 { Vieįllarđ luxurieux: adultère,
   { paįllard, putier, laſcif, ruffien.

Quatre choſes ſont dommageables pour ſe trop haſter.

1 AV combat, ou à la guerre.
2 A gourmandiſe, eţ jeu d'haſard.
3 A un banquet, ſi on n'y eſt appelé.
4 A parler, ou arraiſonner avec un foļ.

Nul ne doibt empeſcher ces quatre choſes.

1 QVi ſe veuļt légitimemenţ marier.
2 Qui va à l'eſcħole.
3 Qui veuļt aider l'oppreſſé.
4 Qui d'une mauvaiſe vįe, meſchante,
   diſſoluë, vicieuſe, ſe retournę à vertu.

En cinq choſes il ne ſe fait pas bon fier.

1 EN un chien eſtranger.
2 En cheval de louäge.
3 En une fame babillarde.

4 *Vnto a proud feruant.*
5 *Vnto the deepeft place of a riuer.*

One lendeth not lightly thefe three things.

1 **H** *Is vvife.*
2   *His good horfe.*
3 *His armes.*

One repenteth not to haue obeyed thefe three things.

1 **V** *Nto the truth.*
2   *Vnto good counfell.*
3 *Vnto the earlie cocke.*

Three things cannot be without fpot.

1 **A** *Potter.*
2   *The vvheele of a cart.*
3 *He vvhich vfeth vvicked companie.*

Of fiue things one ought not to be curious.

1 **H** *Ow another mans houfhold is ruled.*
2   *Of the gouernment and fecret of God.*
3 *Of fifhes meate.*
4 *Of great Lords fecrets.*
5 *Of the change of the vvorld.*

4 En ſerviteur glorieux.
5 En un riuage creux.

On ne preſte pas voluntiers ces trois choſes.

1 SA fame.
2 Son bon cheval.
3 Sès armes.

On ne ſe repent point d'avoir obeï à ces trois choſes.

1 A La verité.
2 A bon conſeįl.
3 Au coᵹ du matin.

Trois choſes ne peuvent eſtre ſans ſouilleure.

1 VN potier.
2 La rouë d'un chariot.
3 Qui converſȩ avec lês̨ meſchanṭs.

De cinq choſes on ne doibt eſtre curieus.

1 COmmenṭ va le meſnage d'auḽtruy.
2 Du gouvernement eṭ ſecreṭ de Dieu.
3 De la viande dês̨ poiſſons.
4 Dès ſecreṭs̨ dês̨ granḓs ſeįgneurs.
5 De la mutacion du tans.   *temps*

Of three things one ought alwayes to remember.

1   *F the commandements of God.*
2 O *Of the good turnes receiued.*
3 *Of the dead, that we may follow*
       or ſhun their ſayings and doings.

Vpon theſe foure things the way is ſlipperie.

1   *Pon the ice.*
2 V *Vpon the dung and moiſt place.*
3 *Vpon report and ambition.*
4 *Vpon a womans beautie.*

Theſe foure things be white, and the fift doth ſhine ouer all.

1   *He ſnow.*
2 T *Siluer.*
3 *VVhite lead.*
4 *The gray haires.*
5 *A ſimple and round heart.*

Three things proper vnto a Counſeller.

1   *Cience.*
2 S *Beneuolence.*
3 *Libertie in ſpeech.*

De trois chofes on fe doibt touf-jours fouvenir.

1 Dès commandements de Dieu.
2 Dès benéfices qu'on a recçuz.
3 Dès tref~paffez, afin d'enfuyvre,
  ou éviter leurs diçts et faiçts.

Sur ces quatre chofes le chemin eft lubrique.

1 Sur la glace.
2 Sur le fient et lieu humide.
3 Sur bruit et ambicion.
4 Sur beauté de fame.

Ces quatre chofes font blanches, et la cinquiefme reluit fur tout.

1 La neige.
2 L'argent.
3 La cerufe.
4 Lès cheveux gris, blançs, chenus.
5 Vn cœur fimple et rond.

Trois chofes propres à un Counfeiller.

1 Science.
2 Benévolence.
3 Liberté en parler.

Things vnprofitable vnto husbandrie.

1 A *Hen without egs and chickens.*
2   *A barren fow.*
3 *An vnfaithfull feruant.*
4 *A fluggifh iourneyman.*
5 *A fleeping cat.*
6 *A whoring woman.*
7 *A fat maidferuant.*
8 *Obftinate children.*
9 *A purfe without money.*

Foure things ought alwayes to be at home.

1 T *He hen-rooft.*
2   *The chimney.*
3 *The cat.*
4 *The good wife.*

Things againft nature.

1 A *Faire maiden without a louer.*
2   *A merchant towne without theeues.*
3 *An old vfurer without money.*
4 *A yong man without ioy.*
5 *An old barne without mice.*
6 *A fcald head without lice.*
7 *An old he goate without a beard.*
8 *A fleeping man decked with learning.*

Chofes inutiles en mefnage.

1 VN poule fans œufs et poulfins.
2 Vne truye ftérile.
3 Vn feruiteur defloyal.
4 Ouvrier pareffeux.
5 Vn chat endormy.
6 Vne fame ribaude.
7 Vne fervante gras.
8 Enfants obftinez.
9 Vne bourfe fans argent.

Quatre chofes doibvent touf-jours eftre en la maifon.

1 LE poulaillier.
2 La cheminée.
3 Le chat.
4 La fame.

Chofes contre nature.

1 VNe belle fille fans amy.
2 Ville merchande fans larrons.
3 Vn vieil ufurier fans argent.
4 Vn jeune home fans lyeffe.
5 Vn vieil grenier fans fouris.
6 Vne tefte tigneufe fans poulx.
7 Vn vieil bouc fans barbe.
8 Vn home endormy orné de fcience.

He that seeketh after these things
loseth his labour.

1 A *Fat hog among the Iewes.*
2   *Truth among hypocrites.*
3 *Loyaltie in a flatterer.*
4 *Sobernesse in a drunkard.*
5 *Monie in a prodigall man his house.*
6 *VVisedome in a foole.*
7 *Great riches in a Schoolemaster.*
8 *A fine wit in a fat bellie.*
9 *Vertue in euill companie.*

These things agree well
together.

1 A *Cutpurse, and a purse*
      full of money.
2 *A runner and a plaine way.*
3 *Goodfellowship and mirth.*
4 *An asse and a miller.*
5 *An host and a glutton.*
6 *A faire woman and faire apparell.*
7 *A shamelesse woman and a cudgell.*
8 *A babe and a good dug.*
9 *Rebellious children and a whip.*
10 *A theefe and a gibbet.*
11 *A good scholer and his bookes.*
12 *Lent and fishmongers.*
13 *Priests and a rich man deceassed.*

Qui cerche ces chofes
perd fa peine.

1　GRaş pourceaux entre lès Juiſs.
2　Verité en un ḫypocrite.
3　Loyauté en vn flateur.
4　Sobrieté en vn yvrongne.
5　Argenţ chez un prodigue.
6　Sageſſę en un foḷ.
7　Grandeş richeſſes en un maiſtre d'écḫole.
8　Entendemenţ ſubtil en un groş ventre.
9　Vertu en mauvaiſe compagníe.

Ces chofes s'accordent
enfemble.

1　VN coupeur de bourſes, eţ une bourſe
　　　　pleine d'argent.
2　Vn courreur eţ chemin uny.
3　Bonne companíe eţ resjouïſſance.
4　Vn aſne eţ un muſnier.
5　Vn ḫoſte eţ un gourmanḍ.
6　Vne belle famę eţ beaux abillemenţs.
7　Vne famę esḫontée eţ un baſton.
8　Vn petit enfant eţ une bonne mammelle.
9　Enfanţs rebelles eţ le fouët.
10　Vn larron eţ un gibet.
11　Vn eſcḫolier eţ ſèş livres.
12　Le careſmę eţ lèş poiſſonniers.
13　Lèş preſtres eţ un riche defunçt.

Thefe things agree not together.

1 A Coward, and the warre.
2 A good iourneyman, and he which keepeth backe his hire.
3 Guefts which haue a good ftomacke, and a flouen hoft, or filthie cooke.
4 A little horfe, and a heauie man.
5 A thirftie perfon, and a little pot.
6 A good hunter, and fluggish dogs.
7 Dogs and cats in a kitchin.
8 A gardiner and a goate.
9 A great cuftome, and poore merchants.
10 An ancient man, and a yong wife.
11 A good maifter, and a difciple which fpeaketh too much.

It is not good to brag of thefe things.

1 THat thou haft good wine.
2 That thou haft a faire wife.
3 That thou haft plentie of crownes.

Ces choſes n'accordent point enſemble.

1 VN coärd, et la guerre.
2   Vn bon manouvrier, et celuy qui
            retient ſon ſalaire.
3 Hoſtes qui ont bon appetit, et
        un hoſte qui eſt ord, ou faſle cuïſinſer.
4 Vn petit cheval, et un peſant home.
5 Vn alteré, et un petit pot.
6 Vn chaſſeur, et chiens pareſſeux.
7 Chiens et chats en une cuiſine.
8 Vn jardinier et une chevre.
9 Groſſe gabelle et povres marchants.
10 Vn home ancien et un jeune fame.
11 Vn bon maiſtre, et un diſciple qui
        parle trop.

Il ne ſe fait pas bon vanter de ces choſes.

1 QUe tu as de bon vin.
2   Que tu as une belle fame.
3 Que tu as force eſcuz.

Of all the mem-
bers of a mans
bodie.

De tous les mem-
bres du corps de
l'home.

A Man
a woman
a tall man
a tall woman
a perſon
people
folkes
the ſoule
the bodie
it is a body without ſoule
a long man
a long woman
a ſhort man
a ſhort woman
a little man
a little woman
a fat man
a fat woman
a leane man
a leane woman
a groſſe man
a groſſe woman
a ſlender man
a ſlender woman

VN home
une fame
un grand home
une grande fame
une perſonne
le peuple
lés gens
l'ame
le corps
ceſt un corps ſans ame
un long home
une longue fame
un home court
une fame courte
un petit home
une petite fame
un home gras
une fame graſſe
un home maigre
une fame maigre
un gros home
une groſſe fame
un home menu
une fame menuë

a hard fauoured man	un home laid
a hard fauoured woman	une fame laide
the head	la teſte
the crowne of the head	le ſommet de la teſte
the haires	lés cheveux
the braines	le cerveau
the eares	lés oreilles
an eare	une oreille
the forehead	le front
the face	la face
the eyes	lés yeux
an eye	un œil
the cheekes	lés jouës
the eye-lids	lés paupiéres
the browes	lés ſourcils
the noſe	le nez
the noſtrels	lés narrines
the mouth	la bouche
the tongue	la langue
the teeth	lés dents
a tooth	une dent
the roofe of the mouth	le palais de la bouche
the gums	lés gencives
the iaw	la machouére
the throate	le gofier
the chin	le menton
the beard	la barbe
the backe	le doz
the ſhoulders	lés eſpaules
a ſhoulder	une eſpaule

a mans yard	la verge
the armes	lès bras
an arme	le bras
the hand	la main
hands	lès mains
a finger	un doigt
fingers	lès doigts
the knockles	lès nœuds dès doigts
a naile	un ungle
nailes	lès ungles
the skin	la peau
she hath a white skin	ell'a la peau blanche
a smooth skin	la peau douce
she painteth her face	elle se farde
painting	fard
the sneuell	le morveau
he is snottie	il eſt morveux
go snottie nose	allez morveux
a stinking breath	un punais
the thombe	le pouce
the necke	le cou
a necke of mutton	un collet de mouton
the loines	lès reins
the buttocks	lès feſſes
the arse	le cul
the arsehole	le trou de cul
to geld	chaſtrer
a thigh	le cuïſſe
thighes	lès cuïſſes
the knee	le genouil

to bow the knee	fleſchir le genouil̤
the leg	la jambe
the calfe of the leg	le mol̤ de la jambe
the foote	le pied̤
feete	lèṣ pied̤s
the heele	le talon
heeles	lèṣ talons
the toes	lèṣ arteaux
the ioynts	lèṣ jointes
a bone	un os
bones	lèṣ os
maribone	la mouëlle
the belly	le ventre
the nauell	le nombril
the breaſt	la poitrine
the boſome	le ſ̤ein
the lap	le giron
the breaſt or dug	lèṣ mammelles
the fiſt	le poinğ
I will giue thee a blow	je te bail̤leray un coup̆
with my fiſt	de poinğ
a rib	une coſ̤te
ribs	lèṣ coſ̤tes
a veine	une veine
a ſinew	un nerf
ſinewes	lèṣ nerfs
the pulſe	le poux
feele his pulſe	taſ̤tez ſon poux
the palme of the hand	la paume de la main̤
the ſtomacke	l'eſtomac

{ *the guts*	{ lès boyaux lès entrailles lès inteſtins
the heart	le cœur
the liuer	le foix
the kidney	le rongnon
the gall	le fiel
the panch	la panſe
the ſpittle	la ſalive
to ſpit	cracher
to ſpue	vomir
to ſpit in ones face	cracher en la face
a fart	un pet
to fart	peter
a fieſt	une veſſe
to fieſt	veſſer

you do nothing elſe but
    fart and fieſt
	vous ne faits que
	    peter et veſſer

you ſtinke	vous puez
to ſhite	chier
the hams	lès jarrets
the ankle bone	la cheville du pied

the ſole of the
    foote
	la planque, ou plante du
	    pied

to itch	demanger
an itch	mangezon
ſcab	galle
ſcabbie	galleux
the white ſcall	la tigne
a ſcaldhead	un tigneux

to scratch	se gratter, grater
to pinch	princer, pinser
to filip	chiquenauder
a filip	une chiquenaude
the flesh	la chair
to cough	tousser
the cough	la toux
I haue a cough	j'ay la toux
I am hoarse	je suy enroué
the hiccocke.	le sanglot.

Of the kindred.　　Du lignage.

M*Y great granfather*	M On ayeul
my granfather	mon grand père
my grandam	ma grand mère
my father	mon père
my mother	ma mère
my vncle	mon oncle
my aunt	ma tante
my niece	ma niéce
my nephew	mon nepveu
my cosin	mon cousin
my she cosin	ma cousine
my stepmother, or	ma maratre, ou
mother in law	belle mère
my father in law	mon beau père
my sonne	mon filz
my daughter	ma fille
my sonne in law	mon gendre

my daughter in law	ma belle fille, ma bru
my brother	mon frère
my ſiſter	ma ſœur
my friend	mon amy
friendſhip	amitié
to embrace	embraſſer, accoller
embrace me	embraſſez moy
take me about the necke	accollez moy
a fatherleſſe child	un orphelin
ſhe is fatherleſſe	ellę eſt orpheline
an heire	un héritier
a ſhe heire	une héritiére
to tickle	chatouįller
you tickle me	vouş me chatouįllez
he is tickliſh	il eſt chatouįlleux
do not meddle with	ne vous accointez paş
her, for ſhe is verie	d'elle, car ellę eſt
tickliſh	forţ chatouįlleuſe
a husband	un mary
a wife	une fame
my wife	ma fame
a virgine, or maide	une vierge, pucelle
the maidenhead	le pucelage
ſhe hath loſt her	ellę a perdu ſon
maidenhead	pucelage
my brother in law	mon bęau frère
my ſiſter in law	ma belle ſœur
a mariage	un mariage
a bridegroome	un eſpoux
a bride	unę eſpouſée

a goſſip	un compère
a ſhe goſſip	une commère
a godfather	un parrain
a godmother	une marrine
a godſonne	un filleul
a goddaughter	une filleule
a midwife	une ſage fame
a nurſe	une nouriſſe
to giue ſucke	alaiçter
to ſucke	teter
ſwadling bands	lẹs bandelettes
to be borne	naiſtre
he was borne at foure of the clocke	il eſt nay à quatre heures
he hath got her with child	il l'a engrofsíe
to nouriſh	nourrir
a ſtilborne	un abortif
to get	engendrer
to dance	danſer
to leade the dance	mener la dance
iealouſie	jalousíe
iealous	un jaloux
a cuckold	un coqu
ſhe hath made her huſband a cuckold	ellẹ a faiṭ ſon mary coqu

The dayes of the weeke.

S *Onday*
 Monday
Tuefday
VVednefday
Thurfday
Friday
Saterday
a weeke
a moneth
three moneths
a yeare
halfe a yeare.

Les jours de la fepmaine.

D Imanche
 Lundi
Mardi
Mefcredi
Jeudi
Vendredi
Samedi
une fepmaine
un moys
troys moys
un an
un demy an.

The xij. moneths of the yeare.

I *Anuarie*
 Februarie
March
Aprill
May
June
Julie
Auguft
September
October
Nouember
December.

Les douze moys de l'an.

I Anvier
 Febvrier
Mars
Avril
May
Juin
Juillet
Aouft
Septembre
Octobre
Novembre
Decembre.

Holy dayes.	Les jours de feſte.
CHriſtmaſſe Chriſtmaſſe day	NOël, *or* Noé̆ le jour de Noël
New yeares day	la Circonciſion, le premier jour de l'an, le jour dẻs eſtrenes.
giue me my new yeares gifts.	baillez moy mẻs eſtrẻnes.
Twelfe daie	lẻs Roys, ou l'Epiphanſe.
Candlemaſſe	La Chandeleur
Shroftide	Careſme prenant, Careſme entrant, le mardi gras.
Palme Sunday	Le Dimanche dẻs Rameaux, Paſqueş fleuries.
Eaſter	Paſques
Eaſter day	le jour de Paſques
The Aſcenſion day	l'Aſcenſion
VVhitſunday	la Pentecoſte
Alhollanday.	la Touſſaints.
The number	Le nombre
one	un
two	deux
three	troys
foure	quatre

fiue	cinq
fixe	fix
feuen	fept
eight	huiçt
nine	nœuf
ten	dix
eleuen	onze
twelue	douze
thirteene	treize
fourteene	quatorze
fifteene	quinze
fixteene	feize
feuenteene	dix-fept
eighteene	dix-huiçt
nineteene	dix-nœuf
twentie	vingt

twentie	one two three foure fiue, &c.	vingt	un deux troys quatre cinq, &c.

thirtie	trente
fortie	quarante
fiftie	cinquante
fixtie	foiffante
feuentie	feptante
eightie	octante
ninetie	nonante
a hundred	cent
a thoufand	mille

a million.	un million.
The number	Le nombre
called in Latine	appellé en Latin
ordinalis,	*ordinalis,*
that is to fay,	c'eſt à dire,
going by order: as	allant par ordre: cōme
the firſt man	le premier home
the firſt woman	la premiére fame
the fecond chapter	le fecond chapitre
the fecond place	la feconde place
{ *the third*	{ le tiers, ou
	{ le troyſieſme,
⌈ *the third*	⌈ la tierce,
⎨	⎨ la troiziefme
⌊ *for the feminine*	⌊ pour le feminin
the fourth	le quatrieſme
the fifth	le cinquieſme
the fixth	le fixieſme
the feuenth	le feptieſme
the eighth	le huiçtieſme
the ninth	le nœufieſme
the tenth	le dixieſme
the eleuenth	l'onzieſme
the twelfth	le douzieſme
the thirteenth	le treizieſme
the fourteenth	le quatorzieſme
The thirtieth	Le trentieſme
the fortieth	le quarentieſme
the fiftieth	le cinquantieſme
the fixtieth	le foiſſantieſme

the ſeuentieth	le ſeptantieſme
the eightieth	l'octantieſme
the ninetieth	le nonantieſme
the hundredth.	le centieſme.

L'ORAISON
Dominicale.

The Lords prayer.

NOſtre Père, qui es ès cieux, Ton nom ſoiț ſançtifié. Ton regnę aḑvienne. Ta volonté ſoiț faitę en la terre commę au ciel. Donne nous au-jour-d'ḥuy noſtre pạin quotidien. Eț nouş pardonne noz offences, comme nouş pardonnons à ceuх qui nous ont offencez. Eț ne nous induy point en tentacion : maiş nouş delivre du mal. Car à toy eſț le Regne, la puiſſancę eț la gloire, aux ſiécleş des ſiécles. Amen.

LES DOVZE
Articles de la Foy.

The xij. Articles of the Chriſtian faith.

Enſepvely

IE croy en Dieu le Père tout‿puiſſant, createur du ciel eț de la terre. Eț en Jeſuş Chriſț ſon ſeul Filz noſtre Seịgneur. Qui a eſté concęu du Sạinçt Eſprit, nay de la vierge Maríe. A ſoufferț ſoubş Ponce Pilate, a eſté crucifié, mort eț enſevely. Eſț deſcendu aux enfers, le tierş jour eſț reſſuſcité dèş morțs. Il eſț monté aux cieux, eſț aſſis à la dextre de Dieu le Père touț‿puiſſant. Eț de là viendra juger lèş vifs eț lèş morțs.

reſurrection

Je croy au Sạinçt Eſprit. La ſạinçtę Egliſę univerſelle. La communion dèş ſạinçts. La remiſſion dèş pechez. La reſurreccion de la chair. La vię éternelle. Amen.

Grace before meate.

ALl that is and ſhall be ſet on this boord,
Be the ſame ſanctified by the Lords word.
So be it.

Graces devant le repas.

CE qui eſt mis, et ſera cy deſſus,
Tout ſoit beniſt par le nom de Jeſus.
Ainſi ſoit il.

Grace after meate.

He that is King, and Lord ouer all,
Bring vs to the table of life eternall.

Apres le repas.

Le Roy des Roys, et gouverneur du monde,
Nous paiſſe au ciel, où toute joye abonde.
Amen.

LE V. CHAPITRE
des Actes des Apoſtres.

MAis un home nommé Ananias, avec ſa fame Saphira vendit une poſſeſſion:

2 Et retint une partie du prix, par le conſentement de ſa fame, et en apporta quelque partie, et la mit aux pieds des Apoſtres.

3 Donṭ Pierre dit: Ananias, pourquoy ḫa Satan rempli ton cœur pour mentir au ſ̣aint Eſprit, eṭ retenir du priẓ du champ̃?

4 Ne demouroit-iḷ paṣ du tout à toy? eṭ eſtanṭ vendu, n'eſtoit-il point en ta puiſſance? pourquoy aṣ tu mis cela en ton cœur? tu n'aṣ poinṭ menti aux ḫomes, mais à Dieu.

5 Eṭ Ananias oyanṭ c̣êṣ parolles, cheut eṭ rendiṭ l'eſprit: dont y euṭ grande cṛainṭ̣e à tous ceuẓ qui ouïreṇt c̣ès choſes.

6 Eṭ aucunṣ jeuneṣ compagnons ſe levans, l'oſtêreṇt, eṭ l'emportêreṇt hors, eṭ l'enſeveliṛeṇt.

7 Aḍvint environ l'eſpace de trois ḫeures aprẻs, que ſa faṃe auſſi, ne ſachanṭ ce qui avoit eſté fait, entra.

8 Eṭ Pierre luy dit, Dy moy, aveẓ vous autanṭ vendu le champ chan Eṭ elle dit, Ouy, autant.

9 Adonḍ Pierre luy dit, Pourquoy aveẓ vouṣ faiṭ complot enſemble de tenter l'Eſpriṭ du Seigneur? voici à l'huiṣ lêṣ pieḍṣ de ceulẕ qui ont enſeveli ton mari eṭ t'emporteront.

10 Eṭ incontinent elle cheut auẕ pieḍṣ d'iceluy, eṭ rendiṭ le'ſprit. Eṭ quanḍ lêṣ jeuneṣ compagnonṣ fûreṇt entrez, ilṣ la trouvêreṇt morte, eṭ l'emportêreṇt hors, eṭ l'enſeveliṛeṇt auprẻṣ de ſon mari.

11 Eṭ aḍvinṭ grande cṛainṭ̣e à toute l'Egliſe, eṭ à tous ceuẕ qui ouïreṇt c̣ès choſes.

12 Eṭ par lêṣ ṃainṣ dèṣ Apoſtres eſtoyeṇt faiṭṣ ḅeaucoup̃ de ſignes eṭ marveilles entre le peuple: Eṭ eſtoyeṇt touṣ d'un accord, au portaḷl de Salomon.

13 Eṭ nul dèṣ autreṣ ne s'oſoit aḍjoindṛe à eux, maiṣ le peuple lêṣ avoit en grand'eſtime.

14 Eṭ de plus en plus s'augmentoiṭ la multitude de ceulẕ qui croyeṇt au Seḷgneur, tanṭ d'ḫomeṣ que deṣ fames.

15 Tellement qu'ilz apportoyent lés malades ès rues, et lés mettoyent en licts et lictiéres, à fin que quand Pierre viendroit, au moins son ombre passast sur quelqu'un d'eux.

16 Et aussi une multitude dès villes voisines venoit en Jerusalem, portant lés malades, et ceux qui estoyent tormentez dès esprits immondes: lesquelz tous estoyent guaris.

17 Lors le principal Sacrificateur se leva, & tous ceux qui estoyent avec luy, qui est la secte dès Sadduciens, et furent remplis d'envíe.

18 Et mírent lés mains sur lés Apostres, et lés mírent en la prison publique.

19 Mais l'Ange du Seigneur ouvrit de nuict lés portes de la prison, et lés mit dehors, et dit:

20 Allez, et estans aut temple, annoncez au peuple toutes lés parolles de ceste víe.

21 Lesquelz ayans ouï ce, entrèrent au poinct du jour au Temple et enseignoyent. Et le principal Sacrificateur estant là venu, et ceux qui estoyent avec luy, assemblèrent le Consistoire, et tout l'estat dès Anciens de la nacion d'Israel, et envoyèrent à la prison pour lés faire amener.

22 Mais quand lés ministres y fûrent venus, ilz ne lés trouvêrent point en la prizon: ainsi s'en retournêrent et l'annoncêrent,

23 Disans: Nous avons bien trouvé la prison fermée avec toute diligence, et lés gardes qui estoyent dehors deuant lés portes: mais quand nous l'avons ouverte, nous n'avons trouvé personne dedans.

24 Le Sacrificateur, et le *Maistre du Temple, et lés *Ou Capitaine* principaux Sacrificateurs ayans ouï ces paroles, estoyent en doubte d'eux, qu'il en seroit fait.

25 Or quelqu'un vint, eṭ leur annonça diſant, Voila lẻṣ ḫomeṣ que vous avieẓ mis en priſon, qui ſont au temple, eṭ enſeigneṇṭ le peuple.

26 Adonc le maiſtre du templẹ avec lẻṣ miniſtreṣ s'en alla, eṭ lẻs amena ſanṣ violence: car ilẓ craignoyeṇṭ le peuple, qu'ilẓ ne fuſſeṇṭ lapidez.

27 Quanḍ ilẓ lẻs eûreṇṭ amenez, ilẓ lẻṣ preſentêreṇṭ au Conſiſtoire. Eṭ le principal Sacrificateur lẻs interroga,

28 Diſant: Ne vous avonṣ nouṣ paṣ defendu par exprèṣ commandement, que n'enſeṣgniſſieẓ point en ce nom-ci? eṭ voici, vous aveẓ rempli Jeruſalem de voſtre doctrine, eṭ vouleẓ remettre ſur nouṣ le ſanꬶ de ceſt ḫome cy.

29 Eṭ Pierre reſpondit avec lẻs Apoſtres, eṭ dîreṇṭ, Il fauṭ pluſtoſt obeïr à Dieu, qu'aux ḫommes.

30 Le Dieu de noẓ Pères ḫa reſſuſcité Jeſus, lequel vous aveẓ mis à mort, le pendant au bois.

31 C'eſt celuy que Dieu ḫa eṣlevé par ſa dextre Princẹ eṭ Sauveur, pour donner repentancẹ à Iſraël, eṭ rémiſſion dèṣ pechez.

32 Eṭ nouṣ luy ſommeṣ teſmoinꬶṣ de cẻṣ parolles, eṭ meſme le Sꬶint Eſprit, lequel Dieu ḫa donné à tous ceuẋ qui obeïſſeṇṭ à luy.

33 Eṭ ayans ouï cela, crevoyeṇṭ d'ire: eṭ conſultoyeṇṭ pour lẻṣ mettṛẹ à mort.

34 Mais un Phariſien nommé Gamaliel docteur de la Loy, ḫonorablẹ à touṭ le peuple, ſe levant au Conſiſtoire, commanda que lẻs Apoſtres ſe retiraſſeṇṭ un peu dehors.

35 Puiṣ leur dit: Homes Iſraëlites, aḍviſeẓ de cẻs ḫomes ce que vous avez à faire.

36 Car paravanṭ cẻṣ jours cy ḫa eṣté Theudas, ſe diſant

eſtre quelque choſe, auquel s'adjoingnit un nombre d'homes, environ de quatre cens: lequel ha eſté occis, et tous ceux qui avoyent creu à luy ont eſté deſtruicts, et reduits à rien.

37 Aprèſ luy s'eſt levé Judaſ Galiléen èſ jourſ de la deſcripcion, et deſtourna groſ peuple apres ſoy: et ceſtui-cy auſſi eſt peri, et tous ceux qui avoyent conſenti à luy, ont eſté deſconfiſs.

38 Et maintenant je vouſ dy, deportez vouſ de cès homes, et lèſ laiſſez: car ſi ce conſeil ou ceſt œuvre eſt dès homes, il ſera deſfait:

39 Mais s'il eſt de Dieu, vouſ ne le pourrez deſfaire, afin que ne ſoyez trouvez eſtre répugnans à Dieu. Et ilz furent de ſon opinion.

40 Et appelêrent lès Apoſtres, et aprèſ lès avoir battus, leur commandêrent qu'ilz ne parlaſſent point au nom de Jeſus: et lèſ laiſſérent aller.

41 Et s'en alloyent joyeux de devant le Conſiſtoire, pource qu'ilz avoyent eu ceſt honneur de ſouffrir opprobre pour le non d'iceluy. *nom*

42 Et touſ lèſ jourſ ne ceſſoyent au temple et par chacune maiſon d'enſeigner et annoncer Jeſuſ Chriſt.

ORAISON.

Père miſericordieux, qui ne deſireſ point la mort, maiſ pluſ⁓toſt la converſion et vie du pecheur: eſtanſ ta grace, bonté et juſtice ſur nous, pour enſevelir touteſ noz iniquitez: afin qu'eſtans environnez de ta bonté, nouſ-nous ejouïſſions en toy, et cheminions en toute droiture, comme nous ſommes enſeignez par ton Filz Jeſuſ Chriſt. Amen.

La benediccion de Moyſe ſelon que noſtre Seigneur avoit ordonné en la Loy.

L E Seigneur vous beníę eţ conſerve: Le Seigneur face luire
ſa face ſur vous, eţ vous ſoit propice: Le Seigneur
retourne ſon viairę enverş vous, eţ vouş mąintiennę en bon
proſperité. Amen.

Si mundus ſaperet, luſus, rixdſque, jocóſque,
Baſia & amplexus ſperneret, & choreas.

TRAICTE DES DANSES,

Avqvel est monftre qu'elles font commę
acceſſoires eꞇ dependanceȿ de paillardiſe :

*Où en paſſant il eſt touché comme les jeus font annexeʒ au rang
d'icelles : & l'abus d'iceux ne doibt eſtre entre les Chreſtiens.*

IE ne fay point de douþte qu'auꝇcunes (entre lėȿ mꞵinȿ
deſquelʒ, parviendra ce petit traiçté) ne m'eſtimeꞇ plꞇin
de grand loiſir, d'avoir enterprins ceſt argument à deſduire :
lequel, à leur aꝺvis, n'eſt pas auꝇtremenꞇ de grandę importance.
Car ja foiꞇ que lėȿ danſes foyeꞇt approuvées, ou condamnées :
ou bien qu'elles foyeꞇt mifes au ranǧ dės choſes indifferentes :
on peuꝇt facilemenꞇ juger felon leur opinion, que cela n'apporte
grand profit ou dommagę à noſtrę république Chꞵreſtienne :
attendu qu'il y a dėȿ poinçtȿ de pluȿ grand poiꝺȿ eꞇ confequence, qui troubleꞇt lės efpritȿ de mꞵinteȿ genȿ doćtes,
efpouventeꞇt lėȿ confcienceȿ dės infirmes eꞇ fimples, qui au-
royeꞇt pluȿ grand befoin d'eſtrę efclarcis eꞇ mis au net, que
de s'amufer, à efcrire contre lėȿ jeus eꞇ danſes. Ouꝇtre‿plus,
on auroiꞇ bꞵeaucoup aꝺvancé fi tout eſtoiꞇ fi bien reformé, qu'on
en fuſt venu jufques auꭓ danſes : c'eſt à dire, que touꞇ ce qui
eſt corrumpu, eꞇ lės abus qui onꞇ la voguę entre lėȿ Chꞵreſtiens,
fuſſeꞇt tellemenꞇ retrenchez, eꞇ ce corꞵs tanꞇ malade tellemenꞇ
reſtabli en fon entier, qu'il ne reſtaſt pluȿ qu'à décider dėȿ
bals eꞇ danſes. Il fe trouvera unę auꝇtre maniére de genꞇs,
qui ne feronꞇ caȿ de fe mocquer de ceſte matiére : commę
ꞵinfi foit, que le mondę eſt plꞇin de mocqueurs, de gens ſanȿ

pieté, fanȝ Dieu, eṭ fanȝ religion. Or quant à ceuȽx-cy, ilȝ
ne meriteṇt auȽcune refpōce, d'autanṭ qu'ilz fe raȽlleṇt auffi
toſṭ dêȿ principauȽȽ poinçṭȿ de la religion Cḫreſtienne, eṭ de
ce qui appartienṭ directement au fervice divin, cōme dês
chofeȿ de moindre confequence: ạinfi ne me foucianṭ poinṭ
bȩaucouꝑ du jugemenṭ de telȿ juges, je lêȿ lairray courir
avau leauë, la bride fur la teſte. Mais quant auȽ premiers,
pour ce qu'ilȝ ne fonṭ du touṭ malinǧs, j'efpère qu'ayanṭ
refꝑondu à leurs objeccions, eṭ declairé lêȿ raifonȿ qui m'onṭ
pouȽfé à defchiffrer ceſte matiére, ilȝ jugeronṭ mon labeur
n'avoir eſté du tout inutile.

Il eſṭ donc à fouhaiter en premier lieu, que lêȿ troubleȿ
pacifiez, eṭ touteȿ diffencions affopíes, lês efpriṭs foyeṇt
affeureȝ de ce qui appartient à leur falut. Touteȿ‿fois, noſtre
Seigneur nous a fufcité un fiecle fi perfeçt en toutes fciences eṭ
fçavoir, auquel tanṭ de genṭȿ doçtes eṭ d'excellentȩ érudicion
fe fonṭ fi ḫeureufement employez à nous enfeigner la maniére
de bien vivre, lês uns en une forte, lês auȽtres en l'auȽtre, que
ceuȽ qui n'en fonṭ poinṭ fatif‿faiçts, n'en doiꝑveṇt imputer
la fauȽte qu'en euȽ‿mefmes.

En aprês, touȿ lêȿ bonȿ doiꝑveṇt defirer, que ceuȽȽ qui
metteṇt la mạin à la reformacion dêȿ mœurs, le fȩiffeṇt à fi
bonnes enfeignes, qu'il ne reſtaſṭ qu'un bien peu à corriger.
Ce fouhait, touteȿ‿fois, ne doiꝑt empefcher le deffȩin de ceuȽȽ
qui tafcheṇt à arracher lês ḫerbeȿ nuifantes au chan du
Seigneur, tanṭ petites foyeṇt elles: comme je fai en ce petiṭ
livret, felon le talent, eṭ lêȿ graceȿ qui me fonṭ eȿlargieȿ
d'enhauȽt.

Joinçt, que fi on confidére meuremenṭ ceſte matiére, j'efpère
qu'on ne la trouvera fi ſtérile, eṭ de petitȩ édificaciō, qu'elle

doibvç eſtre meſpriſée, ou foulée aux pieds. Car beaucoup
de perſonnes de qualité, voirç en la compagnie de notables
perſonnages, de nom et authorité, ne font conſcience de
demander, s'il eſt mal faict de danſer: en demandants un
paſſage formel de l'eſcripture, par lequel il apparoiſſe que lès
danſes ſoyent prohibées et deffenduës: aultrement ilz ne penſent
point mal faire en danſant. D'aultres paſſans plus oultre: et
allegans, ou pluſ toſt abuſans de quelques paſſages de l'Eſcripture, où il appert que lès fidelles ont ſaulté et danſé, ilz
penſent bien avoir trouvé la febvç au gaſteau: comme ſi
c'eſtoit une couverture propre pour couvrir l'infeccion de *l'infection*
leurs danſes.

Conſideré donc que pluſieurs faillent lourdement en ceſt
endroit, poſſible par faulte d'eſtre ſuffiſamment inſtruicts et
informez en ceſte matiére, je lès ay d'aultant voulu ſoulager
en ceſte queſtion, en tant que j'eſpère de profiter au commun,
que auſſi voulant ſatisfaire à aulcuns, leſquelz m'en ont inſtam-
ment requis.

Pour reſpondre donques à ceulx qui demandent un paſſage
formel de l'Eſcripture, auquel lès danſes ſoyent defenduës,
qu'ilz ſachent qu'il y a pluſieurs choſes maulvaiſes, leſquelles
ne font point notammant exprimées en l'Eſcripture pour eſtre
defenduës: toutef fois elles font de meſme eſpêcç et nature,
ou dès dependances d'aulcunes, qui y font exprimées: et
ſoubz leſquelles elles doibvent eſtre compriſes: ou bien quand
le cōtraire d'icelles eſt loué et recommandé, nous ſommes
aſſez inſtruicts de lès rejetter comme condamnées par le
Sainçt Eſprit, d'aultant qu'il y a meſme raiſon ès choſes
contraires.

Au rang dès premiéres, je mettray lès jeus et danſes: lès Le jeu d'hazard.

jeuȿ di-je, par leſqueȽz on attirȩ à ſoy l'argenȶ de ſon prochȧin.
On me dira que quanḍ on jouë, on ne le faiȶ que pour plaiſir
eȶ paſſe‿temp̌s. Voire, maiȿ voulonȿ nouȿ preſter l'oreillȩ à
ce qu'en dit un certȧin autȟeur de noſtre temp̌s: lequel intro-
duiſanȶ deuȼ perſonnageȿ parlans enſemble touchant ceſte
matiére, l'un d'euȼ dit: Eȶ que veuȽt dire le Poëte, qu'Ennuï
s'eſt affublé de la robe de plaiſir? Il ſignifie, reſponḍ l'autre,
que touteȿ les choſeȿ que lès ȟomeȿ prennenȶ pour plaiſir,
leur apportenȶ ennuï eȶ faſcherſe: eȶ cela procède par ce que
lèȿ plaiſirȿ du monde ne font autre choſe qu'ennuis, veſtus
eȶ couverȿ d'un petiȶ de douceur: de laquelle couverture
eſtanȿ lès ȟomeȿ trompez, ſe mettenȶ à le cercher, eȶ en la fin
y trouvenȶ pluȿ de douleur, que douceur. Pour exemple de
quoy, je te parleray ſeulemenȶ d'une choſe, que lès ȟomeȿ
mettenȶ entre lèȿ plaiſirs, par ce qu'il eſt commun à tous
eſtaȶs: ce le jeu: qui certainemenȶ n'eſt autre choſe que le
meſmȩ ennuï: eȶ neantmoinȿ lès ȟomeȿ le prennenȶ pour
plaiſir. Tu veux, peut eſtre, dire la perte, eȶ non paȿ le jeu:
car comme l'on diȶ communemenȶ, il faiȶ bon jouër, mais il
faiȶ mauvaiȿ perdre. L'un eȶ l'autre ſont mauvais: encor que
la perte ſoiȶ pire: pour ce que touteȿ lès choſeȿ qui troublenȶ
le repoȥ de l'eſpriȶ de l'ȟome, ſont mauvaiſeȿ de ſoy. Or encor
que la gȧin ſemble tenir quelque choſe du bon pour eſtre
vȩu utile: il altère, touteȿ‿fois, lès eſpriȶs dès ȟomes, voirȩ
en telle ſorte, que bien ſouvent il leur faiȶ faire pluſieurs
choſeȿ digneȿ de reprehenſion: eȶ bien qu'il donne quelque
fois certȧine joyȩ à ſon ȟome, neant‿moinȿ telle joyȩ n'eſt
poinȶ vraymenȶ bonne, ſi elle ne·procède de ce qui ſe doit
appeler bien. OuȽtre ce, le gȧin faiȶ faire pluſieurȿ deſpenſes
inutiles eȶ en vȧin: eȶ de là vienȶ que qui ſuit le jeu, la à fin

devienṭ povre. Car combien qu'il luy puiſſe aḍvenir de re-
gaịgner autanṭ qu'il a perdu unҫ autre fois, ſi ne luy reviēt-il
jamaiṣ touṣ frais rabatus à la ſomme perduë: eṭ pourtant il
ſemble que tous ceuӿ qui s'y amuſeṇt, faceṇt treṣ⌣mal. Je ne
ſuy paṣ de ceſte opinion, diṭ l'autre, pour ce que j'en ay vҫu
pluſieurṣ qui n'avoyeṇt rien, leſquelʑ touteṣ⌣fois en vivoyeṇt.
Ouy bien aprѐs y avoir employé touṭ ce qu'ilz avoyeṇt. Car
le jeu faiҫṭ propremenṭ comme le lyairre, lequel s'acrochant
à un bon mur, ne ceſſe jamaiṣ juſques à ce qu'il l'ayṭ prѐṣ⌣que
touṭ miné: puiṣ quanḍ le mur eſṭ prѐṣ de tomber en ruine,
il le ſouſtient: ạinſi faiṭ le jeu, quand il s'attachҫ à un ḥome
qui a quelque bien, il fait tanṭ qu'il le deſtruit: eṭ puiṣ quand
il n'a pluṣ rien, il le ſuſtante: pourtanṭ que ce povre mal⌣ḥeureux
hantanṭ lѐṣ lieux où lon jouë, ſe recōmandant eṭ flattanṭ celuy
qui gaịgne, tire de là treṣ⌣vilemenṭ, mais au mieuӀx qu'il
peuӀt, dequoy vivre. Touteṣ⌣foiṣ croy moy mon amy, que le
jeu eſṭ de pluṣ grandes infélicitez que le mal⌣ḥeur de l'ḥome
luy aiṭ poinṭ apportées: eṭ ceſte maudite peſtҫ a tant infeҫté
touṭ le monde, que la pluṣ parṭ dѐs ḥomes (ayāṣ laiſſé à parṭ
lѐs autreṣ maniéres de vivre honeſtes eṭ louäbles) ne font autre
choſe que jouër: eṭ ſe trouve de ceuӿ qui s'enyvreṇt tāṭ
d'iceluy, eṭ y perdeṇt tellemenṭ la lumiére de raiſon, qu'ilz
oublieṇt ḥonneur, leur propre ſalut, leur bien, leur fames,
lѐs enfans, lѐs amis, finallement eux-meſmes: eṭ cōſumanṭs
ạinſi lѐs choſeṣ neceſſaires à leur víe, ſe laiſſeṇt chҫoir en une
pouvreté tant ignominieuſe, qu'ilz craigneṇt pluṣ que lѐs auӀtres
ḥomeṣ lѐṣ voyeṇt, que nouṣ ne faiſonṣ d'eſtre vҫuṣ par lѐs
chiens enragez: eṭ principalemenṭ ſe cacheṇt de ceuӿ qui lѐṣ
coǧnoſſoyeṇt lors qu'ilz eſtoyeṇt en meịlleur eſtat: eṭ neanṭ⌣
moinṣ ne laiſſeṇt paṣ touſ⌣jourṣ de penſer d'où ilʑ pourront

attraper quelque denier, pour le porter jouër, pluſtoſt que
de l'employer en choſe neceſſaire. Maintenant voiſ lèſ beauſ
plaiſirſ qu'ont lès homes en leur jeu d'hazard: eſ non ſeule-
menſ lèſ jouëurs, mais auſſi ceuſ qui s'amuſent à lèſ regarder.
Outre touteſ leſquelles incommoditez, ou pluſ-toſt malheurs,
qui ſuivenſ lèſ jeus: lèſ jouëurs, contre-viennenſ au com-
mandemenſ de Dieu, eſ à la charité enverſ leurſ frères. Que
ſi on me diſ que le jeu n'eſt poinſ defendu par la ſainſtſ
eſcriſture: je reſponſ qu'il eſt vray que nouſ ne trouvonſ
pas en l'Eſcriſture, Tu ne jouëraſ point: maiſ nouſ trouvonſ
bien, Tu ne deſroberaſ point. Or que gañner l'argenſ d'autruy
au jeu, ne ſoit un larcin touſ manifeſte, nul de ſain jugemenſ
le vouldra nier. Car celuy qui a gagné, à quel tiſtre peuſt-il
dire que tel argent eſt ſien? Certeſ quanſ nouſ gagnonſ
l'argent, ou le bien de noſtre frère, il fauſ que ſe ſoit à la ſuëur
de noſtre front, eſ que noſtre labeur luy apporte quelque
profit: eſ tout ainſi que nouſ receſvonſ le bien d'iceluy, auſſi
faut-il que de noſtre induſtriſ eſ travail il reçoive quelque
émolument. Or quand on a tiré ſon argenſ par le hazard
du jeu, je vouſ prie quel profit eſ commodité luy en revient-il?
Il eſt donc à conclurre que c'eſt eſpèce de larcin, laquelle,
encore qu'elle ne ſoiſ pas expriméſ en l'Eſcriſture ſainſte,
neantſmoins elle doiſt eſtre r'apportée au huiſtieſme commandement, où il eſt dit, Tu ne deſroberaſ point. Parquoy
afin que je concluë en brief c'eſt argument: je renvoyſ le

Voy Martyr
en ses lieux
Communs,
au tiltre des
jeux.

Leſteur, auſ lieuſ Communſ de Pierre Martyr, au traité, ou
tiltre dèſ jeux: afin que par le teſmoiñnage d'un tel Doſteur,
nous apprenions à deteſter eſ fuïr touſ jeuſ d'hazard: eſ au
contraire nous exercer en tels exerciſeſ qu'il nouſ meſ là devanſ
lèſ yeux, eſ qui ſéeſt à vrayſ Chreſtiens.

Le ſemblable eſt dèſ danſes, leſquelleſ nouſ pouvonſ
mettrę au premíer eṭ feconḍ rang̃. Car combien que nouſ
n'ayons aucune deffencę expreſſe, où il foiṭ dit: Tu ne danſeraſ
point: ſi avonſ nous un commandemenṭ formel, Tu ne paịl-
larderaſ point: auquel lêſ danſes fe doiḅveṇṭ rapporter. Que Definicion
fi on me demande que ceſt que dêſ danſes? Je reſpondray, des danſes.
confideré la vogue qu'elles ont au-jour-d'ḥuy entre nouſ
Cḥreſtiens, que ce ne fonṭ que geſtes impudiques eṭ diſſoluz,
par leſquelz, la cupidité de la chair eſt reſveịllée eṭ emflambée,
tant ès ḥomeſ qu'èſ fames. Or ſi l'ḥoneſteté eṭ modeſtíę eſt
requiſę aux accouſtremenṭs, comme nouſ voyonſ qu'elle eſt
recommandéę au Deuteronome: eṭ qu'auſſi Sạinṭ Paul en *Deut.* 22.
fon Epiſtre à Tite veuḷt, qu'il y ait une contenance ſạinçte, *Tit.* 2.
ſinguliérement auẋ fames, qui font ordinairemenṭ forṭ curieuſes
en leurs ḥabiṭs: il eſt certạin qu'il y a du venin caché fouḅz
l'ḥerbe. Eṭ quę ạinſi foit, S. Pierrę en fa premiére Canonique
deffenḍ que lêſ fames apparoiſſeṇt eṭ fe monſtreṇṭ par leurs 1. *Pet.* 3.
apparel eṭ attours: joinṭ qu'en pluſieurs autreſ lieux, la
diſſolucion en accouſtremenṭs eſt condamnée, comme pro-
vocans à paịllardiſę eṭ lubricité: à pluſ forte raiſon lêſ geſteſ
diſſoluz, qui fe fonṭ par lêſ propreſ membreſ du corṗs,
doiḅveṇṭ eſtre retrenchez eṭ bannis d'entre lêſ Cḥreſtiens.
Eṭ S. Jude nous exḥorte d'avoir meſme en haine la robe qui
eſt fouịllée par la chair: entendanṭ fouḅz ceſte figurę eṭ
maniére de parler, tous allèchemenṭs, qui nouſ peuveṇṭ attirer
à quelque pollucion eṭ fouịlleure: que deḅvonſ nouſ juger
au priẋ de la chair meſme, qui eſt tellemenṭ poluë, qu'elle
produiṭ fa polucion par dêſ geſteſ vilạins eṭ deſtḥoneſtes? Eṭ
quanḍ Sạinṭ Paul aux Ephéſiens, eṭ Coloſſiens, nouſ defenḍ *Ephef.* 4.
toute parolle faṣle eṭ infeĉte, n'y a-il pas, pour le moins, autanṭ *Coloſſ.* 3.

d’occaſion, voire plus, de condamner lę̃ geſteş diſſoluz? Car
quant auχ parolleş desḩoneſtes, elles ſonţ recueįllieş de noz
oreįlles ſeulement: maiş quant auχ geſteş viląins eţ indagues,
ce ſont autanţ d’objeţs à noz yeuļx, comme ſi on nouş pre-
ſentoit un tableau, auquel toute vilenníę eţ infeccion fuſţ
pourtraiçte. Or que la veuë ne ſoiţ de touş noz ſens celuy
qui a pluş de forçę à nous incliner à polucion eţ ordure, je
n’en veux auļtre juge que noſtre Sauļveur luy⌣meſme quand
il a proféré de ſa bouche, que celuy qui a jetté l’œil ſur la
fame de ſon prochąin pour la convoiter, eſţ deſ⌣ja paįllarḑ
en ſon cœur. Voy-là auſſi pourquoy S. Jeḩan en ſa premiére
Canonique, avec la concupiſcence de la chair, met la concupiſcence dẽs yeuļx.

Math. 5.
1. Iehan 2.

Finalement, quanḑ Sąinţ Paul entre lẽs effeçţş que la grace
de Dieu doiḃţ produirę en nous, meţ la ſobrieté, ou attrem-
pance, ne deffend il pas aſſẽʒ touteş diſſolucions, legiéretez
eţ deşbordemenţs, tant en noʒ mœurs, qu’en noʒ geſtes eţ
auļtre maniére de faire?

Maiş d’auļtanţ que touş lẽs argumenţs ſonţ fondez ſur la
définicion que j’ay donné dę̃ danſes, eţ que quelques unş
me la pourroyeņt nier, il fauţ reſpondrę à ce qu’ilz ont accouſtumé d’objeƈter à l’encontre. Premiérement, j’en ay ouï qui
nieņt lẽş danſes eſtre geſtes impudiques eţ diſſoluz: pourtanţ
que lorş qu’ilz danſeņt, ilʒ ne le fonţ que pour une recréacion
eţ exercice corporel: meſme qu’ilz en uſeņt comme d’une
choſe, laquelle de ſoy n’eſţ bonne, ny mauļvaiſe. Maiş qu’il
ſoiţ reſpondu à telleş genţs en ceſte façon: aſſavoir que leur
affeccion ne peuļt changer la nature de la choſe, qu’elle ne
retienne touſ⌣jours ſon propre nom. Nouş voyonş que ſi
auļcun entre dans un bordeau, voire ſans affeccion d’y paįl-

larder, neant moins le lieu ne lairra point d'eſtre appelé
bordeau. Semblablement qu'ilz diſent qu'en danſant ilz n'ont
aulcune affeccion impudique ou vilaine, ce que toutef-fois ne
ſe peult bonnement croire, car s'ilz n'ont aulcune mauvaiſe
affeccion en danſant, ilz la peuvent avoir, et eux et les aſſiſtans :
mais ſi eſt-ce que pour tout cecy, lès danſes ne laiſſent d'eſtre
appelées geſtes impudiques et vilains.

Mais quoy ? Il n'eſt pas ſeulement queſtion de leurs perſonnes, ains, d'une choſe, laquelle ne doibt eſtre en aulcun
uſage entre lès Chreſtiens. Et que ce n'eſt pas tout d'avoir
ſeulement eſgard à ſoy-meſme, mais il faut regarder à noz
prochains. Qui eſt celuy qui oſe aſſeurer lors qu'il danſe,
ou après avoir danſé, qu'il n'ait provoqué la cupidité de la
chair en quelqu'un dès aſſiſtants ? Mais que ainſi ne ſoit, je ne
produiray qu'un ſeul example, pour en prouver l'effeçt : ceſt,
que la fille et ſœur d'un Conte d'Angleterre, s'amouracha
d'un fort ſimple Gentil home, pour l'avoir veu danſer en la
Cour : ie l'appelle Gentil home de ſang, mais de faiçt, villain
en ſes mœurs et condicions : lequel elle imprima ſi bien en
ſon entendement, que contre le vouloir de père et mère,
parens et amis, elle l'eſpouſa. Maintenant venons au poinçt :
qui incita ceſte ieune dame, riche, ſage, doéte, belle et de
bonne grace, à aimer un home bas, peu diſcret, indoéte,
eſcervelé : voire qui ne ſçait eſcrire ny lire ſon nom, et oulte
plus, fort laid de face et viſage, ſi non le ſeul danſer, et pour
veoir en luy je ne ſçay quel exercice à courir la bague ?

On me dira, qu'elle ne monſtra pas ſa ſageſſe, d'avoir
choiſi ſon mary à la ſeule danſe : mais qu'eſt ce que la chair
n'attire et allèche à ſès laçs ? Car encores qu'il y ait autant de
differences entre lès deux parties, qu'entre le fin or et le plomb,

ou bien entre la vertu, et le vice: meſme que par ſa prudence, elle le refreind de battre, tuer, et getter la maiſon par lês feneſtres, par la moindre mouſche qui luy paſſe devant lês yeulx, ſi eſt-ce qu'il la gaigna par le moyen ſuſ-diçt. Toute-fois s'il n'advenoit pis de la danſe, cecy ſeroit à ſupporter. L'on ſçait bien qu'elle s'en eſt repentíe deſpuis, et non ſans cauſe, mais il faut qu'elle face de tel vin, telle ſoupe. Qui vouldra veoir plus amplement dês mariages contractez par le moyen dês danſes, liſe Pierre Martir en ſês lieux Communs, au tiltre dês Danſes.

Or ſi celuy replique, qu'il ne ſe ſoulcíe point que penſent lês aultres, pourveu qu'il n'y ait rien de maulvais en luy: icy nous voyons le ſcandale donné, et le lien de charité rompu et violé.

Car poſé le cas, que la danſe fuſt miſe entre lês choſes indifferentes pour ſon regard: à cauſe d'une choſe indifferente et legére, a-il deu bailler occaſion d'achoppement à ſon prochain? Mais tant s'en faut que lês danſes ſe doibvent mettre au rang dês choſes indifferentes, qu'on lês doibt tenir pour du tout meſchantes et illicites: de ſorte que je renvoy à leurs conſciences, tous ceulx qui diſent n'avoir aulcune affeccion impudique en danſant. Car une choſe ſi vilaine et ſi infecte de ſa nature, comme eſt la danſe, il eſt impoſſible que celuy qui en uſe, n'en ſoit infecté: ne plus ne moins qu'il eſt poſſible de toucher quelque ordure, et n'en eſtre point ſaſli, infecté et ſouillé.

Et pour plus grande confirmacion de noſtre definicion, nous infererons icy lês Epithetes de la danſe, receuillis dês plus fameux autheurs qui en ont eſcrit, tant Poëtes que Orateurs. Danſe folle, amoureuſe, plaiſante, ſolacieuſe, gaillarde, tremouffante, bafteleufe, chanfonniere, mefurée, trepignante, joyeufe, invitale, publique, nombreufe, gaye, rouänte, infenfée, lafcive, orgienne, nopciere, morifque, fautelante, follaftre, œilladiere, tournoyante, populeufe, bacchique, affemblée, branlante, muette, Venerienne, badine, fingerie, ou fingiere, ridicule, frenetique.

Qu'il ne foit ainfi, recherchons un peu l'origine dès danfes, et nous trouverrons, qu'on n'en peult donner meilleure définicion ne plus propres Epithetes, que celles qui ont efté amenées cy deffus. Car fi nous nous en voulons rapporter à ceulx qui ont efcript dès antiquitez tant dès Grecs que dès Romains, et mefme à quelques Poëtes, nous verrons comme lès danfes ont pris leur origine dès Payens et Ethniques: lefquelz en ont premiérement ufé, lors qu'ilz facrifioyent à leurs dieux. Car eftants plongez ès tenébres fort efpeffes, après avoir forgé dès dieux à leur fantafie, ilz ont penfé qu'iceulx fe debvoyent delecter et plaire en mefmes voluptez et plaifirs aufquelz ilz fe delectoyent. Dont il ne faut doubter que ce ne fuft le Diable qui lès conduifoit: auquel toute fuperfticion, faulfe religion, et erronée doctrine plait fur toutes chofes, quand tel fatras eft accompagné de toute lafciveté et vilennie. Or que telle maniére de faire dès Payens, n'ait efté enfuivíe par lès enfants d'Ifraël, alors qu'ayants facrifié au veau d'or ilz fe mirent à jouër, l'Efcripture nous en fait foy en Exode trente-deuxiefme chapitre.

L'origine des danfes

En après on a commencé à danfer aux jeus et fpectacles publiques, def-quelz toute‑fois lès fames eftoyent chaffées, de peur qu'elles ne fuffent contraintes d'y veoir chofe deshonefte à leur fexe.

Defpuis que par intervalle de temps, toute honefteté et

honte, on̯t commencé à s'eſvanouïr, alorȿ lêȿ filles e̯t fames ont eſté receuës au̯x danſes: il eſt vray que c̦e a eſté à part e̯t en privé.

Finalement aprêȿ quelque eſpace, on s'eſt deſ-bordé juſqueȿ là, que lês ḫomes e̯t fames on̯t danſé peȿle meȿle, e̯t ſinguliére-ment au̯x convives e̯t banque̯tz: en ſorte que nouȿ voyons que ceſte meſchante couſtume s'eſt eſtenduë juſques à nous, e̯t a encoreȿ la vogu̦e au-jour-d'ḫuy pluȿ que jamais. Voila l'origine dêȿ danſes avec leur frui̦ts e̯t proprietez: que s'ilz ſon̯t bien conſidere̯z de ſa̦in entendement, on ne trouvera pas eſtrange que je lêȿ condamne, ayan̯t meſme de mon coſté tan̯t l'autḫorité dêȿ docteurȿ de l'Egliſe, comme dêȿ Péres, qui ſe ſont trouvez en certa̦inȿ Conciles anciens.

Aug. contre Petilian chap. 6.

Sa̦inc̦t Auguſtin au livre contre Petilian parl̦e en ceſte façon: Lês Eveſques avoye̯nt touſ‿jours accouſtumé de réprimer lêȿ danſe̦s vaines e̯t laſcives; mais au-jour-d'ḫuy il y en a au̦cunȿ qui ſe trouve̯nt au̯x danſes, e̯t eu̯x-meſmeȿ danſe̯nt avec lêȿ fames: tan̯t s'en fau̯t qu'il̦z corrige̯nt un tel vice. E̯t ſur le þſeau̦lme trente-deuzieſme, il condamn̦e auſſi lêȿ danſe̦s qui ſe font èȿ jourȿ du Dimanche.

De meſme ſur le Pſeau. 32.

Sa̦inc̦t Jeḫan Chryſoſtome en la cinquante ſixieſme ḫomélie ſur le Genèſe, traic̦tan̯t dêȿ noþceȿ de Jacob, condamne for̯t lêȿ danſes, lês appellan̯t diaboliques. Le ſemblable ſe trouve en la quaranțe ḫuic̦tieſme ḫomélie. Et ſur le quatorzieſme chapitre de Sa̦inc̦t Mattḫieu, parlan̯t de la danſe de Salomé fille d'Herodias, il dit, que quand il ſe faițe une danſe la cive, le diable danſe quant e̯t quant. Au Concile de Laodicée qui fut tenu l'an troys cen̯ts ſoixanțe ḫuic̦t, il fu̯t faic̦t un Canon en cêȿ propreȿ mo̯ts:

Chryſoſt. en la 56. Ho-mel. ſur le Geneſ.

Chryſoſt. ſur le 14. chap. de S. Matth.

Il ne fau̯t poin̯t que lêȿ Cḫreſtienȿ qui vont au̯x noþces,

ballent ou danſent: maiş que chaſtement ilz ſoupent ou diſnent,
comme il eſt ſeant et convenable aux Chreſtiens. Semblablé-
ment en l'an ſix cents ſeptante ſix, fut tenu le ſixieſme Concile
de Conſtantinople, où lês danſeş fûrent defenduës, principale-
ment dêş fames, comme grandement dommageables.

Le troiſieſme Concile de Tolete condamne la perverſe
couſtume dêş peuples, qui s'ocupoyent aux danſeş vilaines et
infectes: et ſur tout, ès jourş du Dimanche et Feſtes, lorş
qu'ilz devvoyent s'employer à ſervir Dieu.

Suivant cèş Canons, aux Eſtats derniérement tenus à Orleans,
au bas aage de Charleş neufieſme, fut faict un article, auquel
(entre autres choſes) eſt defendu à touş jugeş de ne permettre
aulcuneş danſeş publiques èş jourş de Dimanche et feſtes
ſolennelles. Mais en premier lieu, il ſeroit à deſirer, que ceſte
ordonnance fuſt eſtroiçtement obſervée: Secondement, qu'elle
fuſt pluş géneralle, aſſavoir, qu'elle deffendiſt totalement lêş
danſes, comme choſeş meſchantes et illicites. Car ſi nous
ſommeş Chreſtienş de faict, nouş ne devvonş point permettre
que leş povres et aveugleş payens, nous ſurmontent en honeſteté
et modeſtie. Nouş trouvonş qu'entre lêş Romains ceulx qui
eſtoyent par trop addonnez aux danſes, remportoyent une ſi
grande notte d'infamſe, qu'ilz eſtoyent quelque-foiş reputez
indigneş d'exercer un office public et honorable: comme
appert par la cenſure de Domician, lequel, pour c'eſte ſeule
cauſe, jetta horş du Senat un Citoyen Romain, comme indigne
d'un tel degré d'honneur. Saluſte en ſa Catilinaire parlant
d'une fame nommée Sempronia, dit, qu'elle ſçavoit danſer
trop pluş mignonnement, qu'il n'appartenoit à une fame de
bien. Cicero reproche fort et ferme à Gabinius ſon adverſaire
l'eſtude dêş danſes, comme choſe honteuſe et infame. Il fait

ſemblablę en ſêş Philipiques, contrę Antḥoine: eţ en l'oraiſon
pour Murena il dit, qu'ḥome ſobre ne danſa jamais, n'y à
part, ny en banquet ḥoneſte eţ moderé, ſi d'aḑventurę il n'eſt

infenſé. Varro eſcrit, que Scipion ſouloiţ dire, qu'il n'y avoiţ
point de differencę entre un furieux eţ un danſeur: ſauf que
ceſtuy cy eſtoiţ furieux ſeulement quand il danſoit, eţ l'auḽtre
l'eſtoiţ pour toute la víe. De là vienţ le proverbe Latin, que
lêş danſeurş folatreņt, mais c'eſt avec meſure.

Icy nouş voyons évidemment en quellę eſtimę eſtoyeņt lêş
danſes entre lêş Payens eţ infidelles: leſſquelz, pour vray, n'en
pouvoyeņt juger auḽtrement: je parle de ceuﱢ qui avoyeņt le
mejlleur eţ plus ſạin jugement, eţ qui pouvoyeņt peſer eţ
confiderer tanţ lêş danſeş meſmes, que leurs effeçţs eţ fruiçţş
tanţ précieuﱢ. Car ſi c'eſt apreş lêş convives eţ banqueţş, quę
ordinairement on ſe met à danſer, eţ lorş que lês ḥomes ſonţ
plein de vin eţ viandes, ilz ſont adonc plus époinçonneﱢ par
lês aguillonş de la chair, à quoy ſerveņt telles ſorteş de geſtes,
ſinon pour manifeſter leur intemperance? Que ſi on veuḽt
r'apporter cela à l'exercice corporel, ce ſeroit troꝑ ſottemenţ
faiçt: car le corꝑş pour ſa ſanté ne requierţ poinţ d'eſtrę ạinſi
agité eţ vanné incontinent aprêş le repas, de peur d'empeſcher
la digeſtion, comme lêş Mẽdecinş le metteņt en leurş reigleş
de diette. D'avantage, puiş qu'on ſe peuḽt exercer en bẹaucouꝑ
d'auḽtreş maniéreş d'exerciſe, celuy, ce me ſemble, monſtrę
ouvertemenţ qu'il n'a modeſtíe ny temperance, ny ſa ſanté
meſmę en recommendacion, qui choiſiſt lêş danſes pour ſon
exercice. Lêş danſes, donc, n'eſtoyeņt jadis, eţ ne ſonţ pour
le preſent, qu'une pure vilenníe, eţ un teſmoignage treſ⸿certain
eţ treſ⸿évidenţ de l'ordurę eţ intemperance de ceuﱢ qui s'y
deleﬆeņt. Or qu'ainſi ne ſoit, le proverbe François en faiţ

foy: De la panfe, vient la danfe: et fi nous ozions y adjoufter paillardife leur fille aifnée, nous trouverions qu'elle fuit incontinent après. Ce que nous verrons aifément, fi nous confiderons lès effects de la danfe, et lès plus ordinaires. Qui fut caufe que Herodes promift fi legérement à celle belle danfereffe *Mat.* 14. Salomé fille d'Herodias, jufques à la moitié de fon Royaume, *Mar.* 6. finon que par fon danfer vilain et impudique, elle avoit attizé la concupifcence d'iceluy, qui eftoit def-ja un vilain paillard et putier infame, que la volupté et plaifir qu'il y print, l'incita à vouloir faire une recompenfe tant exceffiue? Au furplus, regardons de près en Genèfe, ce qui eft efcript de Dina fille de Jacob, et nous trouverrons que lès danfes fûrent en partie la caufe de fon raviffement. Car combien qu'en ce lieu là il ne foit fait mencion expreffe dès danfes, fi eft-ce que quand il eft dit, que Dina s'enalla veoir lès filles du païs, il y a quelque apparence que lès filles avoyent cefte couftume de s'affembler pour danfer: et afin qu'en monftrant l'agilité de leur corps, leur beauté et plaifanteries, elles fuffent convoitées dès ieunes homes, comme de faict, Dina le fut par Sichem. Et en noftre temps, ne voit on pas iournellement maintes telles chofes, que lès danfes ameinent? L'example par moy cy devant produict, doibt fervir d'argument à tous lès grands Seigneurs, de retirer leurs filles de telz amorcements. Je ne doubte point que fi celle Dame, de laquelle nous avons parlé cy deffus, euft penfé que fon beau danfeur l'euft fervie de telz metz et viandes, que s'accouplant à toutes, pourveu qu'elles foyent coiffées, il deuft fervir de commun eftalon à toute une ville, il n'eft à doubter, dy je, qu'elle ne l'euft laiffé groupir, luy donnant affez loifir d'en affronter une autre. Mais laiffant tout le refte à part, ne voyons nous pas que la

danſe a couſté ſi chèr à ce ſainçt perſonage eſ grand
prophête de Dieu, qu'elle luy a oſté la teſte de deſſuſ lès
eſpaules?

Par le chemin dèſ danſes, lès enfanţs d'Iſraël onţ voulu
porter honneur à unę Idole, à un vęau d'or, à une choſe
morte, eſ quę euχ-meſmes avoyenţ fonduę eſ forgée, à l'imita-
cion dèſ Payens, leſquelz en telle façon ſervoyenţ eſ hono-
royenţ leurſ dieux. Cèſ choſeſ ne ſont elleſ poinţ ſuffiſantes
à faire fuïr lèſ danſes, eſ inciter le Chreſtien à lès avoir en
abominacion, comme choſes ayant ordinairemenţ ſervi à
idolatríe, provoqué à paillardiſe, aliéné bęaucouρ de filleſ de
bonne maiſon de l'amour eſ faveur de leurſ parenţs? finalemenţ cauſé dèſ meurtres infiniţs? Meurtres, dy je: car en tous
cèſ troiſ paſſages ſus alleguez, nous y trouvonſ touſ‿jourſ la
morţ de quelques uns. En la danſe d'Herodes, la morţ de
Jehan Baptiſte: au raρţ de Dina, Sichem y demeura, ſon pèrę
eſ tous ſès ſubieçts: en l'adoracion du vęau d'or, où lès enfanţs
d'Iſraël danſêrenţ eſ ſaulţêrenţ ſi alaigrement aprês avoir le
ventre plęin, il y en mourut environ troiſ mille, en recompenſe
de leur ſi grand joyę eſ lyeſſe. Si donc nouſ conſideronſ lès
evenemenţs dèſ danſes, eſ lèſ bęauχ fruiçts qu'elleſ produiſenţ,
nouſ n'y penſerionſ jamais, que lès cheveuχ ne nouſ dreſſaſſenţ
en la teſte, meſme quand il eſţ queſtion de danſer. Or pour
autanţ que lèſ lieuχ Communſ de Pierre Martyr ont eſté
n'aguères imprimez en Latin, eſ tranſlatez en Anglois, je
renvoyę le leĉteur Chreſtien à iceux, au tilţre dèſ Danſes:
là il trouverra matiére pour luy ſatisfaire.

Il reſte maintenant à reſpondrę à ceulχ qui ſe veulenţ
ſervir de certąinſ paſſageſ de l'Eſcriρture, auſ-quels il eſţ faiţ
mencion que lèſ fidelles onţ danſé.

Premiérement ilz alléguent ce qui eſt eſcript en Exode, *Exod.* 15. que Marie propheteſſe ſœur d'Aaron, laquelle après que Dieu *verſ.* 1. eut ſubmergé et noyé Pharao et ſon armée en la mer rouge, print un tabourin en ſa main, et eſtant ſuivie dès aultres fames, chanta avec elles un Cantique au Seigneur, comme auſſi Moyſe et lès enfants d'Iſrael en chantoyent un aultre. Le ſemblable, quaſi, ſe trouvé en le premier livre de Samuel, au 1. *Sam.* 18. Chapitre dix-huiçtieſme, aprèş que David eut tué Goliath, *verſ.* 1. pluſieurs fames ſortîrent de toutes lès villes d'Iſraël, chantans et danſans devant le Roy Saul, avec tabours, et rebeçs et aultres harmonieux inſtruments.

Or quand ceulx qui ayment à baller voyent qu'il eſt icy parlé non ſeulement dès danſes, mais auſſi dès tabourins et aultres inſtruments muſicaulx, penſent deſ-ja eſtre en la ſalle du bal, et danſer ſelon la notte que lès meneſtriers leur ſonneront: inferants que l'Eſcripture ſus alleguée fait pour eux, et que par icelle, lès danſes ſont approuvées. Mais ilz ſont bien loin de leur compte, à cauſe que contants ſans l'hoſte, il leur convient conter deux fois. Car il eſt tout certain, qu'il y a autant de differençe entre leurs danſes, et celles deſ-quelles ont uſé lès ſainçts perſonages, qu'il y a entre le mariage et la fornicacion: je veux dire, entre chaſteté, et paillardiſe. Et tout ainſi qu'il n'eſt nullement permis de paillarder, auſſi noz danſes et l'uſage d'icelles, ne peuvent eſtre allouéz ny reçeuz. Mais pour le trencher court, nous ne ſaurions recueillir que aulcune apparence de mal, ſigne de laſciveté et diſſolucion, ſe ſoit jamais trouvée aux danſes dès ſainçts perſonages: ains, tout au contraire, ilz s'y ſont portez avec tel honneur, crainte et reverençe envers Dieu, le tout accompagné d'une honeſteté ſi grande, que rien plus: et au faiçt deſ-quelz, trois points ſont

à confiderer, leſ-quelʒ ne ſe peuveɳt trouver nullement auχ
danſeʒ prophaneʒ de noſtre temɓs.

Le premier, l'occaſion qui lèʒ poulſoit à ce faire, eſtoit une
ſi grande joyɇ qu'ilz avoyeɳt conceuë de la faveur que Dieu
leur avoiɬ monſtré, qu'ilʒ ne pouvoyeɳt tenir cachée, maiʒ
failloiɬ qu'ilʒ la manifeſtaſſeɳt par touʒ lèʒ moyenʒ qu'ilz ſe
pouvoyeɳt adviſer. Ce que David declara au ɓſeaume 68.
diſant: Le Seigneur a baillé l'argument auχ fameʒ qui l'onɬ
chanté. C'eſtoiɬ donc commɇ unɇ accion de graces ſolen-
nelleʒ qu'ilʒ rendoyeɳt à Dieu, le chantantʒ autɦeur de leur
delivrance. Quelle communaulté, convenancɇ ou ſimilitude
peulɬ-il avoir entre la danſe de cès ſainçtʒ pères, eɬ celleʒ que
nouʒ voyonʒ pour le jour-d'ɦuy entre lèʒ Cɦreſtiens? Eſt-il
queſtion lorʒ qu'on danſe, de recognoiſtre lèʒ graceʒ de Dieu,
pour l'en remercier en s'eʒjouïſſant en luy? Quanɗ le gallanɗ
tiendra une fillɇ ou fame par la main, eɬ qu'il fera de beaux
ſaulɬʒ devant elle, eɬ gardanɬ meſure, il ſe remuëra, voltigera,
eɬ gambadera à plaiſir, ne fait elle pas ce pendanɬ la bonne
pipée, jouänt à la moriſque de ſon coſté? Mais, je vouʒ príe,
que peulɬ-il avoir de Dieu, de ſa parolle, d'ɦoneſteté en telle
badineríe? Je me tay de leurʒ propos, devis amoureux, laſciveʒ
communicacions, eɬ aſſignacions ſeulemenɬ cognɇuës à la
Diane. Il eſt vray qu'on me dira qu'il ſe fauɬ reʒjouïr, ce que
je concède, maiʒ non d'une joyɇ mondainɇ eɬ diſſoluë.

Le ſeconɗ poinçt eſt, que tout ainſi que le peuple d'Iſraël
eſtoit inſtruiçt au ſervice de Dieu par pluſieurs cérémonies
eɬ façonʒ de fairɇ extérieures, auſſi quand ilʒ le vouloyeɳt
ɦonorer, eɬ luy rendre quelque deɓvoir, ilʒ ne ſe contentoyeɳt
poinɬ de le faire du cœur eɬ de la bouche, ſi quant eɬ quant ilʒ
n'y adjouſtoyeɳt quelques geſtes externes, pour teſmoigner

Pſeau. 68.

ce qu'eſtoit à l'interieur. Nous avonſ trouvé juſques à preſent,
bien peu d'affinité entre lêſ danſeſ dèſ ancienſ Patriarches, eṭ
gentſ de bien eṭ de Religion, avec celleſ donṭ nous uſons à
preſent. Il eſṭ vray que noẕ danſeurſ lêſ vouḷdroyeṇṭ bien
fairҿ eſgalles, eṭ d'un meſme degré d'honneur : ſauf toute‿foiſ
qu'ilẕ ne ſe contenteṇṭ paſ d'avoir le cœur impudique eṭ vilᶏin,
maiſ qu'ilẕ veuleṇṭ de ſcouvrir leur vergongnҿ eṭ vilennſe par
geſteſ diſſoluz. Oḩ ſi j'oſoye mettrҿ en avant, leſ belleſ mines,
que j'ay veuës en mon tempſ, meſme quand on ſe vouloiṭ
monſtrer frolic en danſant, je feroyҿ leſ mouſcheſ rire : mais,
Motus, mon père nous eſcoute, comme dit la chanſon.

Le troiſieſmҿ eṭ dernier poinçt, nouſ monſtre la façon de
faire dêſ nacions Orientales, geſtes extérieurs eṭ couſtume
reçҿuë : contrairҿ en cela, aux Occidentaulẕ. La raiſon eſṭ,
que chaſcune nacion a touſ-jourſ quelque proprҿ eṭ particuliére
inclinacion que n'a paſ l'autre : oulṭre-plus, ceuẕ qui appro-
cheṇṭ de l'Orient eṭ Midy ſont, à cauſe de la chaleur, pluſ
faciles à s'eſmouvoir, eṭ conſequemment à faire geſtes, que
ne ſonṭ pas ceulẕ du Ponant ou du Septentrion : leſquelz,
à cauſe du froiḏ, ſonṭ pluſ graves eṭ pluſ peſanṭs. De là vienṭ
que l'Italien en ſêſ communicacions, maiſ principalemenṭ s'il
parle d'affeccion, entre-meſle tanṭ de geſtes, que ſi un Angloiſ
l'aperçoiṭ de loin, n'oyant, ny entendanṭ ſêſ propoz, le jugera
inſenſé, ou comme s'il jouöiṭ quelque Comedie ſur un eſchau-
faut : qu'on voye, au contraire, un Alleman en chaire, on
l'eſtimera perclus eṭ impoteṇṭ de tous ſêſ membres.

Eṭ pour confirmer cecy, voyonſ comme lêſ ancienſ Romᶏins,
eſtoyeṇṭ eſlongnez de l'opinion dèſ Greçs : ceulẕ-cy eſtimoyeṇṭ
forṭ lêſ danſes eṭ tous ceulẕ qui ſe ſavoyeṇṭ aider d'un inſtru-
menṭ de muſique : lêſ aulṭres eſtimoyeṇṭ peu ḩonorable, eṭ lêſ

danſes, eṭ lèȿ danſeurs. Icy apparoiſṭ la difference de climaṭs
eṭ dès ḥabitanṭs ſouḅz iceuḷx: de là vienṭ que lès Orientauḷx,
rompoyeṇt eṭ déchiroyeṇt leurȿ robes, quand ilz avoyeṇt
entendu de mauḷvaiſeȿ nouvelles: voyla pourquoy ilz ſe
ve̞auḷtroyeṇt en terre, veſtoyeṇṭ dès ſaçs, mettoyeṇṭ dès cendres
ou de la pouḷdre ſur leur teſtes, meſmeȿ lorȿ qu'ilȥ pretendoyeṇṭ
faire quelque penitence, eṭ manifeſter une douleur intérieure̞
eṭ cachée: touteȿ leſ-quelles choſes ſeroyeṇt trouvéeȿ ridicules
eṭ ineptes, èȿ nacions eṭ peupleȿ de par deçà. Eṭ puiȿ que lèȿ
fameȿ prinſeṇṭ dèȿ tabourins en leurȿ ma̞ins, comme nouȿ
liſonȿ que lèȿ fameȿ d'Iſraël onṭ fait, penſeroit-on paȿ qu'elleȿ
fuſſeṇt horȿ du ſens? Ce que toute-foiȿ n'a point eſté trouvé
eſtrange̞ entre lès Iſraëlites, d'autanṭ que ceſtoiṭ la couſtume
de la nacion. Il eſṭ vray qu'on pourroit auſſi rapporter lèȿ
tabourins, eṭ auḷtres inſtrumenṭs de muſique, aux cérémonieȿ
de la Loy Moiſaïque, leſ-quelles ont eſté abolies à la venuë
de Jeſuȿ Cḥriſṭ: de ſorte qu'au-jour⌣d'ḥuy que nous ſommes
ſouḅz l'Evangile, il en faudroit uſer plus ſobrement, eṭ avec
pluȿ grande modeſtíe: maiȿ touṭ cela n'a rien de commun avec
lèȿ danſeȿ du temp̃ȿ preſent.

Cèȿ troiȿ poinçṭs vuïdez, nouȿ trouvons eṭ voyonȿ claire-
ment, quelle̞ affinité il y a entre cèȿ deuȥ mániéreȿ de danſes.
Noȥ danſeurs allegueṇt encore̞ un auḷtre paſſage̞ au livre dèȿ
Roys, où David ſauḷta eṭ danſa devanṭ l'arche du Seḭgneur.
Maiȿ tanṭ s'en fauṭ que cecy leur ſerve pour ma̞intenir leur
danſes, que je n'en vouḷdroye̞ point de pluȿ propre̞ eṭ pluȿ
formel pour lèȿ rembarrer. Car ſi David euſṭ eu une pareille̞
affeccion en la danſe qu'ilz ont en la leur, aſçavoir de complaire auȥ dames, comme noȥ danſeurs s'eſtudieṇt de plaire
à leur mignardes, Micḥol ſa fame ne ſe fuſṭ jamaiȿ moquée

de luy. Il euſt donc danſé pluſ plaiſamment, eṭ d'une façon
plus agreablę à la chair: eṭ de vray, il l'euſt pęu faire, eſtant
agile de ſa nature, eṭ abile à toutes choſes.

Maiſ la reſponce qu'il fąit à Micħol monſtre bien, qu'il ne
pretendoit auḷtre choſe, ſinon de manifeſter par geſtes extérieurs, la grandeur de la joyę qu'il avoiṭ conceuë en ſon
cœur, à cauſe de la preſence de Dieu. C'a eſté, dit-il, devanṭ
le Seigneur ce que j'en ay fait: il apperṭ par ceſte reſponſe,
que ſon affeccion n'eſtoiṭ point au monde, eṭ qu'il ne ſe
ſoucioiṭ poinṭ bęaucouþ du jugemenṭ de Micħol, eṭ de touſ
lèſ mondąins: d'autanṭ qu'il ne vouloiṭ paſ leur complaire,
ny repaiſtre leurſ beauḷx yeuḷx par ſa danſe. Il fauṭ donc
conclure, que David a condamné la mondanité de ſa famę eṭ
ſèſ ſemblables: meſme qu'ellę en a eſté punie par ſtérilité,
qui s'en eſt ſuivíe: argument évident, que Dieu approuvoiṭ
le faiçt eṭ diçt du Prophéte. Que ſi tous ceuḷx qui fonṭ leur
Dieu dèſ danſes, imprimoyeņt cecy en leur eſprit, ilẓ le
recepvroyeņt pluſtoſt à leur condamnacion, que d'eſtre ſi
effrontez de vouloir abuſer de l'Eſcriþture, pour couvrir leur
ordurę eṭ infeccion. Car c'eſt un ſacrilége troþ deteſtable, de
faire ſervir la vérité ineffable du Dieu vivant, à noz affeccionſ
meſchantes eṭ indagues: joinçt, qu'il punira griefvement touſ
telẓ gaudifleurs, qui prophaneņt ąinſi la majeſté de ſon nom,
eṭ ſa divinité aux Sąinçtes Eſcriþtures. D'avantage, quanḍ
nouſ deſguiſonſ tellemenṭ la nature dèſ choſes, que nous
appellonſ le bien mal, eṭ le mal bien, nouſ nouſ depvons
aſſeurer de la malédiccion de Dieu, prononcée par le Prophête
Iſaye, diſant: Malediccion, dit-il, ſur ceuḷx qui diſeņt le mal
eſtre bien, eṭ le bien eſtre mal: qui metteņt tenêbres pour
lumiére, eṭ lumiére pour tenêbres, qui donneņt choſes amèreſ

pour douȴces, eȶ douȴceȿ pour amères. Or je demande maȧin-
tenant, ſi ceuȴx qui approuveȵȶ leȿ danſes, eȶ lèȿ metteȵt entre
lès choſes indifferentes, ne diſeȵȶ paȿ le bien mal, eȶ le mal
bien? eȶ par conſequent, n'enflammeȵȶ paȿ l'ire de Dieu ſur
euȴx eȶ leurȿ fauteurs?

Touteȿ leſ‿quelles choſes conſiderées, j'eſpère que pluſieurȿ
coǧnoiſſanȶȿ quel mal il y a auȴx danſes, lès abandonneront:
eſtimanȶȿ qu'en ce qu'ilȥ lès ont retenuës eȶ favoriſéeȿ juſques
à preſent, ilȥ l'onȶ pluſ-toſȶ faiȶ par ignorance, que par opinia-
ſtreté. Quant aux auȴtreȿ qui vouȴdronȶ perſeverer en leurȿ
diſſolucions, le Seȧgneur lès en veuȴlle retirer, de peur d'en-
courir ſa fureur eȶ vengȩance qui lès
attend, pour avoir contredit
obſtinément à la verité
tanȶ manifeſte.

Louänge à Dieu.

RVLES
for the Pronvnciation.

VVe call our letters after two
manner of wayes.

The learned fort faith.

a, bé, cé, dé, é, ef, gé,
afh, i, ka, el, em, en, o,
pé, qu, er, eff, té, v, ex,
ygreck, ezed, é tranfhé.

The common.

effe, afhe, elle, emme,
enne, erre, effe, ezède.

The French
i, pronoun-
ced as the
Englifh dou-
ble ee.

WHere you muft take paine to pronounce our, v, otherwife then in Englifh: for we do thinke that when
Englifhmen do profer, v, they fay, you: and for, q, we fuppofe
that they fay, kiou: but we found, v, without any helpe of
the tongue, ioyning the lips as if you would whiftle; and after
the manner that the Scots do found Gud. Sound our, i, as
your two, ee.

Jf the Reader doth find ftrange
that the letters fo marked, ạ ḅ ç ḍ ę f̣
ğ ḥ ị ḷ ṇ p̌ q̌ f̣ ṣ ſ̌t ſ̣t ṭ x̣ z̧,
being not wholly pronounced,
are written and printed,
let him note that they ferue
greatly for the prolation: for if
I take away ſ from thefe words,

paſle, faſle, maſle, peſcheur, paſte,
pale, foule, mankind, fiſher, dough,
maſtin, impoſt, deſlié,
a maſtie, a ſubſidie, looſe,
they ſhall differ nothing from theſe,
palle, falle, malle, pecheur,
a ſpade, a hall, a wallet, a ſinner,
patte, matin, delié,
paw, morning, thin,
which be all pronounced ſhort,
and the other verie long
by reaſon of, ſ: ſo that
I conſume twice as much time in
pronouncing maſle, *as* malle.

Of this figne, ', which in Latine is called Apoftrophus.

WHen you find any word *marked with this token, ', fay* *hardly that it is put in ftead* *of,* a, *or,* e: *therefore we do write*
{ l'obiect, l'Eglife, *for*
{ *the obiect, the Church* :
le obiect, la églife : *So we do* *auoide that gaping, which otherwife* *fhould enfue in pronouncing* a, *and,* e: *which vice our tongue abhorreth* *aboue all other faults.*

Sometime, i, *is taken away by* *the fame marke, but onely when* *this fyllable,* fi, *is ioyned with,* il:
{ *fo in ftead of,* fi il vous plait,
{ *if it pleafe you,*
we write, s'il vouṣ plait.

Markes coniunctiues, and difiunctiues.

⌣ : ⁻.

THis marke ⌣ *at the middeft of the* *word, fheweth that it is* *compounded with two: as*
{ ponṭ⌣levis, chauffe⌣pieḍ :
{ *drawing bridge, fhooing horne*

De ce figne, ', lequel en Latin eſt appelé Apoſtrophus.

QUand vouſ trouveʒ quelque moʈ
marqué de ceʃte marque, ', dites
hardimenʈ qu'ellę eſt miſę au lięu
de, a, ou, e: par quoy nous eſcrivons

{ l'objeƈt, l'Egliſe: pour

le objeƈt, la égliſe: ąinſi nous
évitons ce baallement, lequel autremenʈ
s'enſuivroit en prononçant
a, eʈ, e: lequel vice noſtre languę abḥorre
par deſſuſ toutes autreſ fautes.

Aucune⁀fois, i, eſt oſté par
ceſte meſme marque, mais ſeulemenʈ quanḏ
ceſte ſyllabe, ſi, eſt conjointę avec il:

{ ąinſi au lieu de, ſi il vous plait,

nous eſcrivons, s'il vouſ plait.

Marques conjunƈtives, et disjunƈtives.

⁀: .

CEſte marque ⁀ au milieu du
mot, monſtre qu'il eſt
composé de deux: comme

{ pont⁀levis, chauſſe⁀pieḏ:

but this -, signifieth that two
diuers words ought to be pronounced
together: as

{ que fay-je? où va-il si tost?
what do I? whither goeth he so soon
battes-le tous nud: est-il vray?
beate him all naked: is it true?

What betokeneth these two small prickes vpon a vowell.

ä, ë.

THe vowell *hauing two prickes, is deuided*
from the other going before: as

{ bouë, cloué, touäille, queuë:
mire, nailed, a towell, taile:
you shall not say, bo-vë, clo-vé, que-vë:
but bou-ë, clou-é, queu-ë, &c.

é, Masculine.

WE *do not call,* é, *masculine for*
the respect of any gender, but because
that it is founded liuely: as
dote, lapide, me, te, *in Latine:*
and it is alwaies marked
with this accent, é, *as*

{ bruslé, achevé, fessé,   bonté,   pieté:
burned, ended, whipped, goodnesse, godlinesse:
and by adding another, e, *it shall be called*
e, *feminine, because that it hath*

mais ceſte-cy -, ſignifie que deux
divers mots, doiþvent eſtre prononcez
enſemble: comme

que fay-je? où va-il ſi toſt?

battez-le tout nud: eſt-il vray?

Que ſignifient ces deux petits
points, ſur une voyelle.

ä, ë.

LA voyelle ayant deux points, eſt diviſée
d'avec l'autre qui précéde: comme

bouë, cloué, touäjlle, queuë:

vous de direz pas, bo-vë, clo-vé, que-vë:
mais bou-ë, clou-é, queu-ë, &c.

é, Maſculin.

NOus n'appellons pas, é maſculin pour
l'eſgard d'aucun gendre, mais à cauſe
qu'il eſt prononcé vivement comme eſt
dote, lapide, me, te, en Latin:
et eſt tous~jours marqué
de ceſt accent, é, comme

bruſlé, achevé, feſſé, bonté, pieté:

et y adjouſtant un autre, e, il s'appellera
feminin, à raiſon qu'il n'a

Why, e, fe-
minine is fo
called.

but halfe the found of the other, é: as
tanfée, fouëttée, &c. *where the firſt is*
ſharpe, but the other goeth ſlowly, and
as it were deadly: Engliſhmen do
pronounce eaſily

{ créé,   féé:
{ *he created, he appointed to deſtroy:*
but adding to it an, e, *feminine,*
they find therein great difficultie: as

{ créée, féée:
{ *ſhe created:*
briefly, when you ſhall find two, ee, *together,*
the firſt is maſculine, and the other
feminine: Sometime, é, *maſculine is*
found in the middeſt of the word: as

{ moderément, nommément, aifément.
{ *moderately,   namely,   eaſily.*

VVherefoeuer you find this, e,
at the words end, it is an, e, *feminine: as*

{ face,   table,   battre,   dame, une, donne, &c.
{ *a face, a table, to beate, a Lady, one, giue, &c.*

An eafy way
to pronoûce
e, feminine.

pronounce it as the ſecond ſyllable of
bodely *in Engliſh, or the ſecond of*
facere *in Latin: thereof J aduertiſe*
Engliſhmen to take heed in this

A rule of
weight.

rule, as a rule of weight.

que la moitié du son de l'aultre, é: comme
tansée, fouëttée, &c. où le premier est
aigu, mais l'autre va lentement, et
comme en mourant: lês Anglois
prononcent aisément,

{ créé, féé:

mais en y adjoustant un, e, féminin,
il y trouvent grande difficulté: comme

{ créée, féée:

brief, quand vous trouverez deux, ee, ensem-
ble, le premier est masculin, et l'autre
féminin: Aucune‿fois, é, masculin se
trouve au milieu du mot: comme

{ moderément, nommément, aisément.

En quelque lieu que trouviez cest, e,
en la fin du mot, c'est un, e, féminin: comme

{ face, table, battre, dame, une, donne, &c.

prononcez le comme la seconde syllabe de
bodely en Anglois, ou la seconde de
facere en Latin: dont j'adverty
lês Anglois de prendre egard en ceste
reigle, comme reigle d'importance.

Principall rules.

Two chiefeſt rules to be conſidered in the French tongue.

The firſt
principall
rule for the
true reading

W*Hoſoeuer will attain vnto the per-*
fection of our French tongue,
which conſiſteth in the true reading and
pronunciation thereof, let him haue a regard
to auoide too much gaping, and
rough ſpeech: the firſt he ſhall eſchue,
if he obſerueth diligently that
when a word endeth with, e, *feminine,*
and the next beginneth by
any vowell, then the ſaid, e, *feminine*
is drowned, and both the words
are ſo ioyned and coupled together,
as if it were but one diction: an example,

{ Ellę ira avec vous: ellę a dit ąinſi:
{ *ſhe ſhall go with you: ſhe hath ſaid ſo:*
pronounce as if it were written
Ell-ira avec vous: ell a dit ąinſi:
{ Mon père eţ ma mere onţ diſné:
{ *my father and my mother haue dined:*
ſay, Mon per-eţ ma mer-onţ diſné, &c.

For as much as our tongue, for the
ſmoothneſſe thereof, is called lingua
mulierum: *let the louer of it take*
paine to auoide all rough pronunciation:
which he ſhall do, if he keepeth

A rule of
two conſo-
nants, and
ſecond chie-
feſt rule.

Reigles principalles.

Deux principalles reigles, remarquables en la langue François.

QUiconque veult parvenir à la perfeccion de noſtre langue Françoiſe, laquelle conſiſtẹ en la vrayẹ lecturẹ eṭ prononciacion d'icelle, qu'il prennẹ eſgard à éviter un trop̣ granḍ baaller, eṭ aſpre parler: il évitera le premier, s'il obſerve diligemmenṭ que quand un moṭ ſe termine par, e, feminin, eṭ l'autre ſuivanṭ ſe commence par aucune voyelle, alorṣ le dit, e, feminin eſṭ mangé, eṭ lèṣ deuẋ moṭs ſont tellemenṭ joinṭs eṭ couplez enſemble, comme ſi ce n'eſṭoiṭ qu'une diccion: exemple

{ Ellẹ ira avec vous: elle a dit ạinſi.

prononceẓ comme s'il eſṭoit eſcript, Ellira avec vous: ella dit ạinſi

{ Mon perẹ eṭ ma merẹ onṭ diſné:

Mon per-eṭ ma mer-onṭ diſné:

   A cauſe que noſtre langue, pour la douceur d'icelle, eſṭ appelée *lingua mulierum:* que l'amateur d'icelle prenne peine de fuïr toutẹ aſpre prononciacion: ce qu'il fera, s'il obſerve

Reigle de
deux con-
ſonnes.

this rule, that vvhen a vvord endeth
vvith a conſonant, and that vvhich followeth
beginneth vvith another diuers
conſonant, leauing the firſt, he muſt
reade the member of the ſentence
vvithout ſtaying at all: as

{ Aimez lès gens de bien,
{ *Loue honeſt men.*

leauing, z, and the two, s, ſay,
aimeӡ lêṣ genṣ de bien.

{ Tout ce qui luit n'eſt pas or:
{ *All that ſhineth is not gold:*

reade, touȶ ce qui luiȶ n'eṣt pas or.

I, and, v, ſometimes be conſo-
nants, as in Latin.

I, *and,* v, *coupled vvith any vowell,*
or vvith themſelues, become conſonants:
and therefore do cauſe the conſonant going
before to be left: v, *alſo is ioyned vvith,* r: *as*

{ Eſtes vous jalous de moy?
{ *Are you iealous of me?*

ſay, eṣteṣ vouṣ jalouӽ de moy?

{ Ce ſont choſes vulgaires, mais vrayes:
{ *theſe be common things, but true:*

reade, choſeṣ vulgaires, maiṣ vrayes.

{ Je ne peuӽ laiſſer ce livre, tant
{ *I cannot leaue this booke, ſo much*
{ j'y trouve de conſolacion:
{ *conſolation I find therein:*

ſay, tanȶ j'y trouve de conſolacion.

ceſte reigle, que quand un moṭ ſe termine
par une conſone, eṭ celuy qui ſuiṭ
ſe commence par une autre diuerſe
conſone, laiſſant la premiére, il fauṭ
qu'il liſe le membre de la ſentence
ſans s'arreſter aucunement: comme

{ Aimez lès gens de bien,

laiſſanṭ le, z, eṭ lèş deux, s, dites,
aimeẓ lèş genş de bien.

{ Tout ce qui luit n'eſt pas or:

liſez, touṭ ce qui luiṭ n'eſṭ pas or.

I, et, v, aucune-fois ſont conſo-
nes, comme en Latin.

I, eṭ, v, couplées avec unẹ autre voyelle,
ou avec elleş meſmes, deviennenṭ con-
ſones: eṭ fonṭ que la conſone qui lèş pré-
cède ſoiṭ laiſſée: v, auſſi joint avec, r: comme

{ Eſtes vous jalous de moy?

dites, eſteş vouş jaloux de moy?

{ Ce ſont choſes vulgaires, mais vrayes:

liſez, choſeş vulgaires, maiş vrayes.

{ Je ne peux laiſſer ce livre, tant

j'y trouve de conſolacion:

dites, tanṭ j'y trouve de conſolacion.

Exception.

M, n, r, *are alwaies expreſſed:*
and moſt often, l, *at the words end:*
neuertheleſſe, m, *at the words end,*
is pronounced as, n: *ſo ſay in ſteed of*
{ champ, nom, faim, temps,
{ *a field, a name, hunger, time,*
chan, non, fin, tans: *and* chans, *for* champs:
ſome ſay in the ſingular number
{ dompté, prompt,
{ *tamed, ready or prompt,*
and by adding, s, *we pronounce*
dontez, prons: *ſauing before an*
other, m, *as* emmonſeler:
and before, b, *as* embellir:
laſtlie before, p, *as* emplir.

And as for, n, *it is not fully ex-*
preſſed in verbes of the third perſon
plurall ending im ent: *as*
{ ilz aiment, aimoyent, aimêrent, &c.
{ *they loue, they did loue, they loued:*
ſay, partlie eating, n,
ilz aimẹnt, aimoyẹnt, aimêrẹnt, &c.

Note this rule.

A*Nd as the Latin maketh long the*
laſt ſillable ſauing one of legêrunt
vel legêre, *ſo we draw long the ſelfe*

Exception.

M, n, r, ſont touſ-jours exprimées:
eţ le plus ſouvent, l, à la fin du mot:
toute-fois, m, en la fin du mot,
ſe prononce comme, n, ąinſi dites au lieu de

{ champ, nom, faim, temps,

chan, non, fin, tans: eţ chans, pour champs:
aucunş diſeņt au nombre ſingulier

{ dompté, prompt:

mais en adjouſtant, s, nouş prononçonş
dontes, prons: ſauf devant unę
autre, m, commę emmonſeler:
auſſi devant, b, commę embellir:
finalemenţ devant, p, commę emplir.

Quant à, n, elle n'eſt paş plainement exprimée auẋ verbeş de la troiſieſme perſonne
du nombre plurier terminée en, ent: comme

{ ilz aiment, aimoyent, aimêrent, &c.

dites, en partie mangęant, n,
ilz aimeņt, aimoyeņt, aimêreņt, &c.

Notez ceſte reigle.

Eţ comme le Latin prononce long la
penultieſme ſyllabe de *legêrunt*
vel legêre, ąinſi nouş tironş long la

same syllable of the third person
plurall of the first tense
perfect: saying,

⎧ ilz aimêrent, ilz conclûrent,
⎪ *they loued,   they concluded,*
⎨ ilz entendîrent, ilz lûrent,
⎩ *they vnderstood, they read,*

drawing the last sauing one verie long.

Another exception.

A Vec, *doth euer*
   sound, c: *as*

⎧ avec toy, avec luy, avec nous:
⎩ *with thee, with him,   with vs:*

f, *is expressed alwayes at the end:*
neuerthelesse, when we find a
word ending in, f, *before we*
pronounce the other following,
beginning with a consonant, we stay
somewhat vpon, f: *as*

⎧ le meschef que tu m'as procuré:
⎪ *the mischiefe which thou hast procured vnto me*
⎨ le bœuf d'Angleterre:
⎩ *the beefe of England:*

do the like when you shall find, ains.

Of, l.

B Ecause *of the vncertaintie of the*
   letter, l, *we can giue*
no generall rule: therefore when it

meſme ſyllabe de la troſieſme perſonne
pluriére de ce premier tempş
perfeçt: diſanţs,

   ilz aimêteņt, ilƶ conclûreņt,

   ilz entendíreņt, ilƶ lûreņt,

continuanţ la penultieſme forţ longue.

Vne autre exception.

AVec, exprime
  touſ⌣jours, e: comme

   avec toy, avec luy, avec nous:

f, eſt touſ⌣jours exprimée en la fin:
toute⌣fois, quanḑ nouş trouvons un
mot terminé en, f, devanţ que nouş
prononcionş l'autre ſuivant,
commençant par une conſone, nouş poſonş
quelque peu ſur, f, comme

   le meſchef que tu m'aş procuré:

   le bœuf d'Angleterre: faiteş le ſemblable

quanḑ vouş trouverez, ạins.

De, l.

A Cauſe de l'incertitude de ceſte
  lettre, l, nouş n'en pouvonş baịller
reigle generalle: parquoy quand elle

is not pronounced, it ſhall be marked
in this ſort, ⸤: *notwithſtanding I*
haue obſerued this, that after, au, *and,* ou,
l, *is neuer expreſſed: as*
au⸤tre, ou⸤tre, &c. *therefore I will*
leaue it behind without writing, or
printing the ſame, although that they ſay
that it ſerueth vnto the quantitie: ſome ſay
⎧coulpable, poulpitre.
⎨*guiltie,   a deske.*

　Sometime, l, *is not pronounced,*
although it ſhutteth vp the member,
or the whole ſentence: which is
ſtrange: for we do ſound
commonly the laſt conſonant
at the end of the member, period,
or when we do interrupt the ſentence
in taking of our breath: as
⎧il eſt ſaou⸤: il monſtre le cu⸤:
⎨*his belly is full: he ſheweth his arſe:*
in ſteed of
⎧un ſol, deux ſols, col, genoil, fenoil,
⎪*a ſhilling, two ſhillings, necke, knee, fenell,*
⎨licol, fol, fols, mol,
⎩*a halter, foole, fooles, ſoft:*
ſay, un ſou, deux ſous, cou, genou, fenou,
licou, fou, fous, mou:
yet we ſay, un eſcu ſol.
d, *verie often is left, as*
⎧vouʒ me bleſſeʒ le pieḑ:
⎨*you hurt my foote.*

n'eſt paſ prononcée, elle ſera marquée
en ceſte ſorte, ꝇ: toute‿foiſ j'ay
obſervé cecy, qu'après, au, eṭ, ou:
l, ne s'exprime jamais: comme
auḽtre, ouḽtre, &c. parquoy je la
lairray derriére ſanſ l'eſcrire, ou
imprimer, encore qu'on die
qu'elle ſerve à la quantité: aucunſ diſeṇt

{ coulpable, poulpitre.

 Aucune‿fois, l, n'eſt point prononcée,
encoreſ qu'elle termine le membre,
ou la ſentence totale: ce qui eſt
eſtrange: car nouſ prononçonſ
couſtumiéremeṇt la derniére conſoṇ
en la fin du membre, periode,
ou quanḍ nous interromponſ la ſentence
reprenaṇt noſtrẹ aleine: comme

{ il eſt ſaouꝇ: il monſtre le cuḽ:

au leu d'un

{ ſol, deux ſolz, col, genoil, fenoil,

 licol, fol, fols, mol:

dites, un ſou, deux ſous, cou, genou, fenou,
licou, fou, fous, mou:
touteſ‿foiſ nouſ diſons un eſcu ſol.
d, bien ſouvent eſt laiſſé: comme

{ vouſ me bleſſeẓ le pieḍ:

g, *and*, t, *ſometimes at the end of the*
point abſolute, are of the like, for
they be not fully pronounced: as

   ⎧ ce brochet eſt de mon eſtanğ:
   ⎪ *this pike is of my pond:*
   ⎨ j'ay coupé mon doig̃t:
   ⎪ *I haue cut my finger:*
   ⎪ *ſay*, du plomb̧: le loup̆.
   ⎩   *lead:*   *the wolfe.*

C, as, ſ.

VV*Hen you find this*, ç, *before*, a, *and*, o,
   pronounce it as, ſ: *as*
⎰ venez çà garçon: maçon:
⎱ *come hither boy: bricklayer:*
ſay, venez ſa garſon: maſſon.

Ch.

VV*E pronounce*, ch, *as Engliſhmen*
   ſh: *ſo in ſteed of*
⎰ choſes, chapitre, cheval,
⎱ *things, chapter, horſe,*
ſay, ſhoſes, ſhapitre, ſheval, &c.
Except all proper names, as Cḩanaan,
Zacḩarie: *with theſe*, cḩolere, cḩorde,
eſcḩole, cicḩorée, *and their deriued.*

g, et, t, aucune‿fois en la fin du
point abfolut, font de mefme, car
ilz ne font pas plainement exprimez: comme

ce brochet eſt de mon eſtang :

j'ay coupé mon doigt :

dites, du plomb : le loup.

C, comme, f.

QUand vous trouvez ce, ç, devant, a, et, o,
prononcez-le comme, f: comme

venez çà garçon, maçon :

dites, venez fa ga garfon, maffon.

Ch.

NOus prononçons, ch, comme lès Anglois
fh: ainfi au lieu de

chofes, chapitre, cheval, &c.

dites, fhofes, fhapitre, fheval, &c.
Exceptez tous noms propres, comme Chana-
an, Zacharie: avec ceux-ci: cholere,
chorde, efchole, cichorée, et leurs derivez.

A generall rule for the quantitie.

N*Ounes ending in*, afe, aife, able, ible, ife,
ofe, ufe, *and* eufe, *be long: as*

Caucafe   fournaife, capable,
a mountains name, fornace,   capable,
poffible, mignardife,
poffible,   wantonneffe,
Mandofe,   cornemufe,   hideufe:
a mans name, an inftrumēt of muſick, dreadful things :
therefore I thinke that it were better to
write it by, z, *becauſe it is a double*
conſonant among the Latins:
ſo it cauſeth the ſyllable where
it lieth, to be long: neuertheleſſe the
vſe is ſuch, that, ſ, *betwixt two vowels*
is ſounded as, z: *except*
refentir, refembler, *for they be*
expreſſed as hauing two, ſſ: *as*

elle refemble fon père: il refent l'ḥéréfie:
ſhe is like her father: he ſmelleth hereſie.
Pronounce this word, prinfe, *and his*
compounds, as written, by, z, prinze.

Exception of this quantitie.

B*Vt if the laſt,* é, *be maſculine,*
the accent is changed:

devalifé,   baptifé, &c.
robbed by the way, baptiſed.

Reigle generalle pour la quantité.

NOmş terminez en, aſe, aiſe, able, ible, iſe,
oſe, uſe, eţ euſe, fonţ lonǧs: comme
Caucaſe, fournaiſe, capable,

poſſible, mignardiſe,

Mandoſe, cornemuſe, hideuſe:

parquoy je penſe qu'il vaudroit mieuҳ
l'eſcrirҿ par, z, à cauſe que c'eſt une double
conſonҿ entre lèş Latins:
ąinſi elle cauſe que la ſyllabe où
ellҿ eſt, foiţ longue: toute‿foiş
l'uſagҿ eſt tel que, ſ, entre deuҳ voyelles
eſt prononcée comme, z: exceptez,
reſentir, reſembler, car ilz
s'expriment commҿ ayantş deuҳ, ſſ, comme
elle reſemble ſon pҽre:
il reſenţ l'ḩéréſie.
    Prononcez ce mot, prinſe, eţ ſèş
compoſez, commҿ eſcriţ par, z, prinze.

ſ, entre deux
voyelles
comme, z.

Exception de ceſte quantité.

OR ſi le dernier, e, eſt maſculin,
l'accent eſt changé: comme
devaliſé, baptiſé, &c.

Likewife if, r, *or,* z, *do end
the diction, the accent is made vpon the
laſt ſyllable: as,* temporiſer,
authoriſez.

Ine.

WOrds *ending in,* ine, *as* cuiſine,
concubine, &c. *ſee that,* i, *be ſome-
what longer then the other ſyllables.*

Ie.

ALſo *words ending in,* ie, *we make
the accent vpon,* i, *as* jalouſie,
Philoſophie, folie, marvoisie.

C, and, g.

VVE *ſound,* c, *and,* g, *as the Latines:
ſo in ſteed of,* ca, co, cu, *we ſay*
ka, ko, ku: ga, go, gu, *as in Engliſh:
but,* ge, *as* je: gi, *as the
firſt ſyllable of* gibet, *in Engliſh.*

Of two, ll.

VVHen *two,* ll, *follow,* ai, ei, oi, *or* ui,
*they be pronounced with the flat of
the tongue, touching ſmoothly the
roofe of the mouth: yong boyes here
in England do expreſſe it verie well
when they pronounce* luceo, *or* ſaluto: *and*

Whē two, ll,
be liquides.

femblablement, fi, r, ou, z, terminent
la diccion, l'accent fe fait fur la
derniere fyllabe: comme, temporifer,
authorifez.

Ine.

MOts terminez en, ine, comme cuifine,
concubine, &c. faites que, i, foit un
peu plus long que lès autres fyllabes.

Ie.

AUffi au mots en, ie, nous faifons
l'accent fur, i: comme jalousíe,
Philofophíe, folíe, marvoisíe.

C, & G.

NOus proferons, c, et, g, comme lès Latins:
car pour, ca, co, cu, nous difons
ka, ko, ku: ga, go, gu, comme en Anglois:
mais, ge, comme, je: gi, comme la
premiére fyllabe de *gibet*, en Anglois.

De deux, ll.

QUand deux, ll, fuivent, ai, ei, oi, ou, ui,
elles fe prononcent du plat de
la langue, touchant doucement le
palais de la bouche: lès jeunes enfans
d'Angleterre l'expriment fort bien
quand ilz prononcent *luceo*, ou *faluto:* et

Englishmen in sounding Collier, *and*
Scollion: *likewise*
the Italian pronouncing voglio, duoglio:
for they do not sound them with the end,
but with the flat of the tongue, as
{ tailler, treillis, quenouille, bouillir:
{ *to cut, a grate, a distaffe, to seeth:*
where you must note that, i, *serueth for nothing*
in words of aill, *and* ouill,
but to cause the two, ll,
to be pronounced as liquides.

Exception.

{ CAvillacion,   ville, tranquille,
{   *a cauillation, a towne, a calme,*
{ anguille, estoille, avillir,
{ *an eele,   starre, to abase,*
with their deriued, be pronounced
with the end of the tongue.

Addition.

ALl *the words ending in,* illon, *as*
{ eschantillon, papillon, coquillon:
{ *a scantling, a butterflie:*
and these following with their deriued
are sounded with the flat of the tongue:

lẻs Anglois en prononçant *Collier*, et
Scollion: femblablement
l'Italien en prononçant *voglio, duoglio:*
car ilz ne lẻs prononcent pas du bout,
mais du plat de la langue: comme

{ tailler, treillis, quenoille, bouillir:

où il faut noter que, i, ne fert de rien
aux mots en, aill, et, ouill,
finon que faire que lẻs deux, ll,
foyent prononcées comme liquides.

Exception.

{ CAvillacion, ville, tranquille,

anguille, eftoille, avillir,

avec leurs derivez fe prononcent
du bout de la langue.

Addition.

{ TOus mots en, illon, comme

efchantillon, papillon, coquillon:
Et ceux qui fuivent, avec leurs derivez,
fe prononcent du plat de la langue:

baaller,	chenille,	fille,
to gape, a caterpiller, a daughter, or maiden,
eſtrille,	petiller,
a curricombe, to tread vnder feete,
fillaſtre,	millet,
a ſonne in law, milet,
filleul, Hillot, coſtillier,
a godſonne, ones armes bearer,
grille,	lentille, canetille, fretiller,
a grediron, a kind of peaſon, edging lace,
Caſtille,	famille,	Cornille,
a proper name, a family, a mans name,
faucille,	tillac,	bille,	killes,
a ſickle, a boord of a ſhip, a bowle, nine pins,
entortiller, abiller,	babiller,
to wind, to apparell, to prattle,
artilleríe,	carillonner,
artillerie, to chime with belles,
perilleux,	eſſoriller,	eſcarbillat,
perillous, to cut ones eares, quicke and liuely.
volatille, formilliére.
*foule,	a mole hill.*

V.

Ecauſe this letter troubleth much
the ſtranger, not knowing when it is
a vowell, or conſonant: I haue cauſed
two diuers, v, to be caſt: ſo, v, conſonant is
marked thus, v: and it is vvritten in the
middeſt of the vvord, vvhere I thinke that other-

baaller, chenille, fille,

eſtrille, petiller,

fillaſtre, millet,

filleul, Hillot, coſtillier,

grille, lentille, canetille, fretiller,

Caſtille, famille, Cornille,

faucille, tillac, bille, killes,

entortiller, abiller, babiller,

artillerſe, carillonner,

perilleux, efforiller, efcarbillat,

volatille, formilliére.

V.

ACauſe que ceſte lettre trouble beaucoup l'eſtranger, ne ſachant quand
elle eſt voyelle, ou conſone, j'ay fait faire
deux differents, v: or, v, conſone eſt
ainſi marqué, v: et le trouverez eſcript au
milieu du mot, où j'ay penſé que autre-

vvife it vvould caufe fome doubt
vnto the reader: fay not
{ v-rayment, yv-ronge, liv-re,
   truly, a drunkard, a booke,
but vray-ment, y-vrongne, li-vre.

Es, and, ez.

THofe *that vvrite,* z, *for,* s : *and,* s,
  for, z, *do erre greatlie: as*
bleffes, *and* bleffez, *do fhew: becaufe they*
differ much: for in
{ tu me bleffes,   tu te trompes,
  thou hurteſt me, thou art deceiued,
es, *is founded after,* e, *feminine, that*
is to fay, deadly: but in
{ vouꟅ me bleffez, vouꟅ me trompez,
   you hurt me,   you deceiue me,
ez, *goeth more fharply, drawing the*
laſt fyllable as if it were in Latine,
but we gape not fo much:
{ mès,   tès,   fès, lès, dès,   excès,   decès,
  mine, thine, his, the, of,   exceffe, deceaffed,
differ much in the pronunciation from the laſt
fyllable of thefe words,
{ ames, hoſtes, chofes, nouvelles :
  foules, gueſts, things, newes :
for fuch diƈions ought to be written
with an open, è, *and to be pronounced*
after the fort that Englifhmen do
found, dayes: *write then,* mès, procès,

ment il pourroiṭ cauſer quelque douḅṭẹ
au leċteur: ne diteṣ pas

{ v-rayment, yv-rogne, liv-re,

mais, vray-ment, y-vrongne, li-vre.

Es, et ez.

CEuẋ qui eſcriveṇt, z, pour, s: eṭ s,
pour, z, faịlleṇṭ grandement: comme
bleſſes, eṭ bleſſez, monſtreṇt: acauſe
qu'ilẕ differeṇṭ bẹaucoup: car en,

{ tu me bleſſes, tu te trompes:

es, eſṭ prononcé en maniére de, e, feminin:
c'eſt à dire, lentement: mais en

{ vouṣ me bleſſez, vous me trompez:

ez, eſṭ plus aigu, prolongẹaṇṭ la
derniére ſyllabe comme ſi c'eſtoit en Latin,
maiṣ nouṣ ne baallonṣ paṣ tant:

{ mės, tės, ſės, lės, dės, excès, decès,

differeṇṭ bẹaucoup en pronunciacion
de la derniére ſyllabe de cėṣ moṭs,

{ ames, họſtes, choſes, nouvelles:

car telle diccions ſe doiḅveṇt eſcrirẹ
avec un, ė, ouvert, eṭ ſont exprimées
ſuivaṇṭ le ſon que lės Angloiṣ
donneṇṭ à, *dayes:* eſcriveẕ donc, mės, procès,

père, mère, frère, eſpèce, Lucrèce,
and diuers others with this, è.

X.

SOund, x, *at the words end, as,* s:
⎰ prix,   paix,   deux, eux,   ſix, dix, yeux, &c
⎱ *a price, peace,   two, them, ſix, ten, eyes,*
as pris, pais, deus, &c.

Exception.

PErplex, *is excepted: neuertheleſſe ſay*
deuzieſme, ſizieſme, dizieſme, ſeizieſme,
ſizẹin: *for* deuxieſme, ſixieſme, dixieſme,
ſeixieſme, ſixẹin, *ſounding,* x, *as,* z:
pronounce exprès, *by,* ſ:
⎰ ſoixante, lexiue, Bruxelles, complexion,
⎱ *ſixtie,   lye,   Bruſſels,   complexion,*
as hauing two, ſſ, ſoiſſante, &c.
otherwiſe, x, *is pronounced as in*
Latine: extraordinaire, exalté.

En, or ent.

WHereſoeuer you find, *en, or,* ent,
ſauing in verbes, ſound it as
betwixt, e, *and,* a: *ſay then (not opening too*
much your mouth, as if you ſhould
pronounce, a, *opened) keeping*
meaſure betwixt, e, *and,* a, *as if one ſhould vvrite*
⎰ antandemant, attantiuemant, &c.
⎱ *vnderſtanding,   attentiuely.*
in ſteed of entendement, attentivement.

père, mère, frère, efpèce, Lucrèce,
e̲t plufieurs autres, avec ce̲ſt, è.

X.

EXprimez, x, en la fin du mot, comme, s:
{ prix, paix, deuꭓ, euꭓ, fix, yeuꭓ, &c.

comme, pris, pais, deus, &c.

Exception.

PErplex, e̲ſt excepté : toutef-fois, dite̲s
deuziefme, fiziefme, diziefme, feiziefme,
fizꭓin : pour deuxiefme, fixiefme, dixiefme,
feixiefme, fiꭓain, fonant, x, comme, z :
prononcez, exprès, par, ſ :

{ foixante, lexive, Bruxelles, complexion,

comme ayan̲s deuꭓ, ſſ : foiſſante, &c.
au furplus, x, e̲ſt prononcé comm̲e en
Latin, comme, extraordinaire, exalté.

En, et, ent.

EN quelque lieu que trouverez, en, ou, ent,
fauf auꭓ verbes, prononce̲s le comme
entre, e, e̲t, a : dite̲s donc (n'ouvran̲t point
trop̲ voſtre bouche, comme fi vou̲s prononciez, a, ouvertement) mai̲s gardan̲t
mefur̲e entre, e, e̲t, a, comme fi on e̲ſcrivoit,

{ antandemant, attantivemant, &c.

au lieu de, entendement, attentivement.

Exception.

NEuerthele$$e you mu$t $ound the$e
by, e, mien, tien, $ien, chien, vient,
and all vvords ending by ien, *or* yen:
pronounce gehenne, *as* genne.

Ai, and, ay.

Ai, hath three diuers pronunciations.

AI, *and*, ay, *haue three diuers $ounds: for
the fir$t per$on $ingular of the future ten$e
of the Indicatiue moode, and the$e three verbes,*
{ ay, *and his compounds:* je $çay,   nay,
{   *I know, I am borne,*
be fully pronounced as, é, *ma$culine:
$ay then for*

Ay, like, é, ma$culine.

{ ay, j'ay, je diray,   je liray, j'aimeray, &c.
{ *I haue, I will $ay, I will reade, I will loue.*
as if it were written, é, jé, je diré, je liré, &c.
  *But the fir$t per$on $ingular of the
fir$t perfect ten$e of the Indicatiue moode,
is $ounded as it is written, as*

Ay, as it is written.

{ j'aimay, je trouvay, je parlay, &c.
{ *I loued, I found,   I $poke.*
  *As for the re$t, where$oeuer you $hall
find* ai, *$ound it as,* gaye, gaping.
  Note that if, e, *followeth immediatly,* ay,
*then the pronunciation
is changed: as,* j'ay, *is $ounded like*
jé: *but when you $ay,*

Exception.

TOuteſ-foiſ vouſ prononcereʒ ceux-cy
par, e: mien, tien, ſien, chien, vient,
eꞇ touſ léſ motſ termineʒ par, ien, ou, yen:
prononcez, gehenne, comme genne.

Ai, et, ay.

AI, et, ay, ont troyſ divers ſons: car
la premiére perſonne ſinguliére du tanſ,
futur de l'indicatif, eꞇ céſ troiſ verbes,

{ ay, eꞇ ſéſ compoſez: auec, je ſçay, nay,

ſont entiéremenꞇ prononcez, comme, é,
maſculin: diteſ donc au lieu de

{ ay, j'ay, je diray, je liray, j'aimeray, &c.

comme s'il eſtoit eſcript, é, jé, je diré, je liré.
   Maiſ la premiére perſonne ſingul, du
premier temp̄ſ perfeꞇ de l'Indicatif,
eſt exprimée commę ellę eſt eſcripte, comme

{ j'aimay, je trouvay, je parlay.

   Quant au reſte, où vouſ trouverez,
ai, prononceʒ le comme *gay, gaping.*
   Noteʒ que ſi, e, ſuit immediatement, ay,
lorſ la prononciacion
eſt changée: comme, j'ay, eſt prononcé
ąinſi que, jé: maiſ quand vouſ dites,

{ combien que j'aye,
{ *though I haue,*
it is almoſt pronounced as if you
ſhould part all the vowels aſunder:
(namely in meeter) as
{ j'a-y-e: abba-y-er: a-y-es.
{ *I haue, to barke, haue thou.*

Oy.

O Y, *as if you ſhould vvrite it ſo,* oè,
vvith an open, è,

{ moyne, moy, toy,   ſoy, foy,   loy,
{ *a monke, I,   thou,   he, faith, law,*
ſay, moène, moè, toè, foè, &c. *adde to it*
all the third perſons plurall of the
preterimperfeĉt of the indicatiue:
but if, e, *followeth,* y, *then it doth alter:*
as moyen, doyen: ſay, mo-y-en.

Ain.

V V E *ſound,* ain, *as,* in: *ſo*
in ſteed of

{ main, maintenant, demain,   ſaint:
{ *hand,   anone,   to morrow, holy:*
ſay, min, mintenant, demin, ſint:
but vvhen, e, *followeth,* n, *the vowell,* i,
goeth more towards, a: *as,*

{ balaine, ſeƥmaine, capitaine, fontaine:
{ *a whale, a weeke, a captaine, a fountaine:*
and to make it more plaine, romain,

{ combien que j'aye,

il eſt preſ~que prononcé comme ſi vous
ſépariez touteſ léſ voyelles à part:
(nommément en carmes) comme

{ j'a-y-e: abba-y-er: a-y-es.

Oy.

OY, comme ſi l'eſcriviez ainſi, oè,
avec un, è, ouvert,

{ moyne, moy, toy, ſoy, foy, loy:

dites, moène, moè, toè, ſoè, &c. adjouſtez y
touteſ léſ troiſieſmeſ perſonneſ pluriéreſ de
l'imperfeçt de l'indicatif:
mais ſi, e, ſeul enſuit, y, lors il ſe change:
comme moyen, doyen: dites, mo-y-en.

Ain.

NOuſ prononçons, ain, comme, in: ainſi
donc au lieu de

{ main, maintenant, demain, ſaint:

dites, min, mintenant, demin, ſint:
maiſ quand, e, enſuit, n, lorſ la voyelle, i,
tire pluſ du coſté de, a: comme

{ balaine, ſeþmaine, capitaine, fontaine: .

et pour le faire plus évident, romain,

certain, vilain, ſouverain, *are*
pronounced as romin, certin, vilin:
but adde, e, *to it, and the pronunciation*
is cleane altered, ſo that, romaine,
is as you ſound, vaine, *in Engliſh,*
and ſuch like, but more ſhorter.

Of gua, gue, gui.

VV*Hereſoeuer you find* gua,
ſound it as the firſt
ſyllable of gallop: gue, *as* geving:
gui, *as* Gilbert, *and ſuch like.*

Exception.

I'Arguë, Guïſe, aiguë, *haue three ſyllables,*
I do argue,   ſharpe:
as j'ar-gu-ë, Gu-ï-ſe, ſentencẹ ai-gu-ë:
eſguïſer, ambiguë, *and* contiguë, *haue foure*
to whet, doubtfull,   adioyning:
as eſ-gu-ï-ſeʐ mon couſteau:
    whet my knife:
c'eſt choſe am-bi-gu-ë:
it is a doubtfull thing.

Of, ſ, in the middeſt of
the word.

FOr *as much as the ſtranger is verie much*
entangled about this letter, ſ, *knowing*
not when it muſt be pronounced
or left, let him marke this rule

certain, vilain, ſouverain: ſont
prononcez comme, romin, certin, vilin:
mais adjouſtez y, e, et la prononciation
eſt totalement changée, en ſorte que, romaine
eſt comme vous prononcez, *vaine*, en Anglois,
et autres ſemblables, mais beaucoup plus court:

De gua, gue, gui.

EN quelque lieu que trouverez, gua,
prononcez-le comme premiére
ſyllabe de *gallop:* gue, comme *geving:*
gui, comme *Gilbert*, et ſemblables.

Exception.

I'Arguë, Guïſe, aiguë, ont trois ſyllabes:

comme j'ar-gu-ë, Gu-ï-ſe, ſentence ar-gu-ë:

eſguïſer, ambiguë, et contiguë en ont quatre:

comme, eſ-gu-ï-ſez mon couſteau:

c'eſt choſe am-bi-gu-ë.

De, ſ, au milieu
du mot.

POur autant que l'eſtranger eſt fort
empeſché par ceſte lettre, ſ, ne
ſachant point quand il la faut prononcer
ou laiſſer, qu'il marque ceſte reigle

for his great eaſe: and all thoſe words
with all their compounds and deriued,
comprehended in this table following,
do ſound, ſ, in the middeſt, and none other
I meane deriued (to teach
the vnskilfull in the Latine tongue) which
do deſcend from one, as from their head
and ſpring: as by example, doer, doing,
done, *do proceed from the Engliſh verbe*
to do: *likewiſe vvhen I haue*
put this vvord conſtruire, *it ſhall ſerue for*
inſtruire, inſtruccion, inſtructeur, con-
ſtruccion: *and ſo,* conſtituer, *ſhall ſerue*
for ſo much as if I had ſpecified deſtituer,
reſtituer, reſtitucion, &c.

J confeſſe that this rule and ſom
others, be as ſuperfluous for this
booke, becauſe that the letters
not fully ſounded, are marked:
but the reader hauing framed his
tongue by the meane of this treatiſe, vvhen
he ſhall reade in another booke without notes,
he vvill remember the better,
vvhen and how he muſt
pronounce, or leaue ſuch letters as
ought to be expreſſed or left.

Now the generall vſe for, ſ, ioyned
vvith a conſonant in the middeſt of the vvord,
is, that all proper names do ſound, ſ:
as Auguſte, Baptiſte, Anaſtaſe, &c.

ſ, ioyned
with a con-
ſonant in
the middeſt.

pour ſe ſoulager: que tous cȩ̃s moţs
avec leur compoſez eţ derivez,
comprins en ceſte table qui ſuit,
exprimeņt, ſ, au milieu, eţ nul autre.

J'entenḑ lȩ̃s derivez (afin d'enſeįgner
l'ignorant en la Latine) leſ-quelz
deſcendeņt d'un, comme de leur ſourcȩ
eţ origine: exemple, *doer, doing,
done*, vienneņt de ce verbȩ Anglois,
to do: ſemblablemeņt quand j'auray
ſpecifié ce mot, conſtruire, il ſervira pour
inſtruire, inſtruccion, inſtruǎeur, con-
ſtrucǎion: eţ ąinſi, conſtituer, ſervira
autaņt comme ſi j'avoyȩ ſpécifié deſtituer,
reſtituer, reſtitution, &c.

Je confeſſe que ceſte reiglȩ eţ quelques
autres ſoņt comme ſuperfluȩs pour ce
livre, acauſe que toutȩs lȩ̃s lettres
aucunemeņt delaiſſées ſoņt marquées:
maįs le Lecǎeur ayant façonné ſa
langue par le moyen de ce livret, quand
il lira en quelque autre livre ſaņs marques,
il ſe ſouviendra bȩaucouꝑ mieux,
quand eţ comment il luy conviendra
prononcer, ou laiſſer tellȩs lettres, qui
ſont exprimées ou laiſſées.

Or la reigle generalle pour, ſ, conjointȩ
avec une conſonȩ au milieu du mot
eſt, que touȿ nomȿ propres exprimeņt, ſ:
comme Auguſte, Baptiſte, Anaſtaſe, &c.

Except.

BAſle, Creſpin, Chriſt, Eſtienne, Eſcoce, *coming from* Baſilia, Criſpinus, Chriſtus, Stephanus: *adde to it* Hieroſme.

Exceptez.

Eſtienne

BAſle, Creſpin, Chriſt, Eſtienne, Eſcoce, deſcendants de *Baſilia, Criſpinus, Chriſtus, Stephanus:* adjouſtez y Hieroſme.

SOVND LIKEWISE ſ,
in theſe here written.

A

ABſconſe
abſterſif
abſtraccion
acoſter
aduſte
agreſte
Alquemiſte
anagrammatiſme
anguſtie
annaliſte
Apoſtolique: *ſay*
neuertheleſſe
apoſtre

apoſtaſie
apoſter
apoſtrophe
apoſtume
artiſte
aſpect
aſperges
aſperger
aſperité: *yet ſay*
aſpre
aſpirer
aſſiſter
aſtres
aſtraindre

aftuce
atefter
auftère
auftrafe
auftruche
Athéifte.

B

Barbarefque
Bafque
bafte
baftille
baftion
baftonades
except bafton:
beftiole
beftialité, fay beftail
befte, and
beftelette
birrafque
bifcaye
bifcarié
bifcuit
blafphémer
bofquet
brufque.

C.

cameriftes
cataftrophe
cauftique
célefte

chafteté
circonfpect
circonftance
cifternes
clandeftinement
cliftère
combuftible
confifcacion
confiftoire
confifte, *with all the
deriued of* fto, ftas: *as*
refifter, affifter, &c.
contefter
confpirer, *and the
compounds of*
afpirer, refpirer, &c.
conftance
conftellacion
confte: *as,* il ne
confte rien de cela
cofmographíe
coftiller
conftipacion
conftruire
contefter
contrefcarpe
contrifter
crépufcule
corufcacion
criftal

crotefque

curialifte

cuftode.

D.

damafquiner

demonftracion *onely*

defaftre

débufquer

defcripcion, *and all the*
fubstantiues in cion,
coming from the com-
pounds of this verbe
Scribo: as infcripciō, &c.

defefpérer

deftituer

deftruccion, *with all*
the compounds of his.

défifter

deftinée

detefter

digefte

digeftion

difcontinuër

difcorder

difcourir

difcrécion

difcrépant

difcuter

difgrace

difparir

difpenfacion

difpofer

difpofte

difputer

diftance

diftamperé

diftillacion

diftinguer

diftique

diftraire

diftribuer

difturber

domeftique.

E.

ecclefiaftique

égeftion

embufcade

enregiftrer

efcabeau

efcabreus

efcalade

efcamper

efcarbillat

efcarbot

efcargot

efcarlatin *only*

efcarpins

efcarfelle

efcopetteríe

efcouäde

eſclave
eſcrimer
eſpace
eſpèce
eſpérance
eſprit
eſquadron
eſtafier
eſtaſe
eſtamel
eſtimer
eſtocade
eſtomac
eſtrade
eſtradioṭs
eſtrapade
eſtropiat
évangeliſte.

F.

fantaſtique
feſtin
fiſcal
fiſque
fiſtule
flaſque
freſquade
friſque
fruſtrer
funeſte
fuſte

fuſtiguer.

G.

garguéſques *or*
garguaſques
gaſtadors
geſtes.

H.

ḥaſpic
ḥerboriſte
ḥiſtoire
ḥiſtrion
holocauſte
ḥoſpitalité *only*
ḥoſtíe
ḥoſtilité.

I.

jaſpe
illuſtrer
impoſture
improviſte
à l'improviſte
inceſte
inconſtant
incruſtacion
indigeſte
induſtríe
ineſpérement
infeſter
infiſter

inspiracion
instable
instaler
instant
instinct
instigacion
instituer
instruire
instrument
intestins
investiture *onely*
juristes
jusques
justice
justifier.

L.

lansquenets
legiste
liste
lustre
lourdesque.

M.

magistrat
majesté
manifeste
masculin
masque
mastic
menstrual
ministre

miste
mistère
mistique
modeste
molester
monastère
moresque *or*
morisque
monstre, *for a monster*
mosquet
mosquée
moustache
moustele
muscade
muscadet
musc
muscles.

N.

non‿obstant.

O.

obélisque
obscur
obstacle
obtester
obstinacion
offusquer
opuscule
organiste
ostade
ostentacion.

P.
Panſioniſtes
papiſtique
paſteur, *except*
paiſtre
paſcal
paſtenades
perſiſter
peſte
piſteau
piſtolet
poſte
poſtérieur
poſtérité
poſtiles
poſtillon
poſtulacion
poſtpoſer
poſtule
poteſtat
phantaſtiquer
prédeſtinacion
prépoſtère
presbitère, *onely:*
preſtiges
priſtin
proſcrire, *except*
  eſcrire deſcrire:
proſpective
proſpérer

proſterner
proſtituer
proteſter.

Q.
queſtion
donner la queſtion
  that is la gehenne
  or torture
  to giue the racke

R.
régiſtre
reſpecter
reſpectivement
reſpirer
reſplendir
reſtaurer
reſte
reſtituer
robuſte
ruſtique
ruſtre.

S.
ſacriſtie
ſatisfaire
ſcholaſtique
ſeneſtre
ſequeſtre
filiquaſtre
ſylogiſme
ſylveſtre

finiſtre
folſtice
fophiſte
ſparme
ſubhaſtacion
ſubſtituer
ſubminiſtrer
ſubſtance
ſugeſtion
ſuſpect
ſuperſticieux
ſuſpendre.

T.

tempeſtatif, *and*
tempeſtative, *onely*
terreſtre
teſtament

teſticule
teſtifier
teſton
teſtonner
   all the compounds of
   trans, *a prepoſition: as*
transfigurer
triſteſſe
turquefque

V.

veſtales
veſtiaire
veſtiges
villanefque
viſcoſité
viſtampanade.

T.

SOmetime we found, t, *as*, f:
chiefly when the diction cometh
from the Latin: the Englishmen do
the like, as, diction, impofition:
neuertheleffe J do write, c, *in ftead of*, t.

Y.

Y, *and*, i, *differ thus: for*, y, *is neuer*
    ioyned with a vowell to be a confonant,
but goeth alwaies alone: as,
{ ayons,   noyau, un tuyau, bouyau,
{ *let vs haue, a kernell, a quill,   a gut*,
you fhall not fay a-jons, *but* a-y-ons:
yet we fay,
{ j'y vay,   j'y penferay.
{ *I go thither, I will thinke on it.*

Gn.

VV E *pronounce*, gn, *almoft as*
     Englifhmen do found, minion:
fo melting, g, *and touching*
the roofe of the mouth with the
flat of the tongue, we fay
mignon, compagnon: *fay then*
campa-gne, *and not* campag-ne.
VVhen the Italian faith guadagno,
bifogno, *he expreffeth our* gn, *verie well.*

T.

AUcune-foiş nouş prononçonş, t, comme, ſ:
principalemenţ quanḍ la diccion
vienṭ du Latin : lês Angloiş fonṭ
le ſemblable : comme, diction, impoſition :
touteş-foiş j'eſcry, c, au lieu de, t.

Y.

Y, eṭ, i, differeṇt aịnſi : car, y, n'eſt jamaiş
joint avec une voyelle pour eſtre conſone, mais il va touſ⌣jours ſeul : comme,

{ ayans, noyau, un tuyau, boyau,

vouş ne diteẓ pas a-jons, mais a-y-ons :
touteş⌣foiş nouş diſons,

{ j'y vay, j'y penſeray.

Gn.

NOuş prononçons, gn, bien prèş comme
lês Angloiş prononceṇt, *minion* :
aịnſi nouş fondons, g, eṭ touchanṭ
le palaiş de la bouche du
plaṭ de la langue nouş diſonş
mignon, compagnon : diteş donc
campa-gne, eṭ non, campag-ne :
quanḍ l'Italien dit *guadagno*,
biſogno, il exprime forṭ bien noſtre, *gn*.

A notable rule.

VVE *enterlace moſt often letters not
neceſſarie, but onely to*
auoide gaping: as
{ Jeḫan ḫa-til diſné?
{ *hath Iohn dined?*
in ſtead of, Jeḫan ḫa-il diſné?
{ que t'a-til fait?
{ *what hath he done to thee?*
for, que t'a-il fait?

Certaine Rules of Syntaxe.

The French article.

VVE *diſcerne a ſtranger by the article, for it is not knowne but
by long vſe, becauſe we haue
no generall rule for to teach it:*
le, *and*, un, *be the articles of
the maſculine gender:* la, *and*, une,
*of the feminine: but in the plurall number
there is no difference.*

To decline a nowne of the maſculine gender.

Singul.

Nom. LE ſoldat, ou, un ſoldat:
The ſouldier, or, one ſouldier.

Vne reigle digne d'eſtre notée.

NOus entrelaçonſ bien ſouvenṭ dèſ lettreſ non neceſſaires, ſeulemenṭ pour éviter le baallement: comme

{ Jeḥan ḥa-til diſné?

au lieu de, Jeḥan ḥa-il diſné?

{ que t'a-til fait?

pour, que t'a-il fait?

Certaines reigles de Syntaxe.

L'article François.

NOuſ coǧnoiſſonſ l'eſtranger par l'arti-cle: car il n'eſṭ poinṭ coǧneu que par long uſage, acauſe que nouſ n'avonſ poinṭ de reigle generalle pour l'enſeiǧner: le, eṭ, un, ſonṭ lès articleſ du genre maſculin: la, eṭ, une, du feminin: mais au nombre plurier il n'y ḥa poinṭ de difference.

A nowne of the feminine gender is thus declined.

Singul.

Nom. LA fame, ou, une fame:
The woman, or, one woman.

Gen.   Du ſoldat, ou, d'un ſoldat:
        Of the ſouldier, or, of one ſouldier.
Dat.   Au ſoldat, ou, à un ſoldat:
        To the ſouldier, or, to one ſouldier.
Accuſ. Le ſoldat, ou, un ſoldat:
        The ſouldier, or, one ſouldier.
Vocat. O ſoldat:
        O ſouldier.
Ablat. Avec le ſoldat, ou, par le ſoldat:
        VVith, or by the ſouldier.

Plurall.

Nom.   Lès ſoldaţs:
        The ſouldiers.
Gen.   Dès ſoldaţs:
        Of the ſouldiers.
Dat.   Aux ſoldaţs:
        To the ſouldiers.
Accuſ. Lès ſoldaţs:
        The ſouldiers.
Voc.   O ſoldaţs:
        O ſouldiers.
Ablat. Avec lès ſoldaţs, ou, par lès, &c.
        VVith the, or by the ſouldiers.

Gen.   De la fame, ou, d'une fame:
        Of the woman, or, of one woman.
Dat.   A la fame, ou, à une fame:
        Vnto a woman, or, vnto one woman.
Accu. La fame, ou, une fame:
        The woman, or, one woman.
Voc.   O fame:
        O woman.
Abl.   Avec la fame, ou, avec une fame,
        ou, par la fame:
        VVith the woman, or, by the woman.

Plurall number.

Nom. Lės fames:
        VVomen.
Gen.   Dės fames, &c. *as in the mafcul.*

La.

THis ſyllable, la, *hath three diuers ſignifications, for moſt often it is an article of the feminine gender: as* la pome: *ſometime a relatiue, as*

> où eſt ma chemiſe?
> *where is my ſhirt?*
> ne la voyez vous pas?
> *do you not ſee it?*
> je ne la voy pas: je la voy:
> *I ſee it not: I ſee it.*

ſometime it is an aduerbe, ſignifying place: then it is ſo marked, là: *and it muſt alwaies in reading be ioyned with the word which goeth before: as*

Là, is read with the word which goeth before.

> ſéez vous-là au bout de la table:
> *ſit you there at the boords end:*

yet we ſay, il eſt là-ſus en paradis: vous jouëz là-dedans à plaiſir.

The difference of, bel, and, beau.

*B*El, *is alwaies put before words beginning with a vowell: as*

> un bel arbre: un bel home, &c.
> *a faire tree: a faire man*, &c.

but, beau, *cometh alwaies before a conſonant, as* beau filz, *a faire child.*

La.

CEſte ſyllabe, la, ḫa troiȿ diverſes
ſignifications: car le plus ſouvanṭ
c'eſt un article du genre feminin: comme
la pome: aucune‿fois un relatif: comme

⎧ où eſṭ ma chemiſe?
⎪
⎨ ne la voyeȥ-vouȿ pas?
⎪
⎩ je ne la voy pas: je la voy:

aucune‿fois c'eſt un adverbe ſignifianṭ
lieu: alors il eſṭ ạinſi marqué, là:
eṭ fauṭ qu'en liſant il ſoit touſ‿jourȿ
joint avec le moṭ qui
prècéde: comme

⎰ ſéeȥ vouȿ-là au bouṭ de la table.

toute‿foiȿ nouȿ diſons, là-ſus en paradis:
vouȿ jouëȥ là-dedans à plaiſir.

La difference de bel,
& beau.

BEl, eſṭ touſ‿jourȿ miȿ devanṭ moṭs
qui ſe commenceṇṭ par une voyelle: cōme

⎰ un bel arbre: un bel ḫome, &c.

mais, beau, vient touſ‿jourȿ devant
une conſone: comme, beau filȥ.

The difference of, je, moy, tu, and toy.

THe*se foure pronounes differ thus:*
je, *is alwaies ioyned with the verbe:*
and, moy, *is abſolute: as if I ſay,*
{ qui ha fait cela?
{ *who hath done that?*
you anſwer, moy, *J:*
and not, je: *except you will*
rehearſe all the clauſe, which is tedious: as
{ je l'ay fait.
{ *I haue done it.*
Tu, and, toy, *are the like: as*
{ qui rit? c'eſt toy:
{ *who laugheth? it is thou:* and not, tu.

Of certaine pronounes poſſeſſiues.

MOn, ma, ton, ta, ſon, ſa, *are of*
like nature as bel, *and* beau:
to auoide the gaping which ſhould
follow, we ſay,
{ mon ame: ton arbaleſte:
{ *my ſoule: thy croſſebow:*
{ ſon hoſteſſe:
{ *his hoſteſſe:*
in ſtead of, ma ame: ta harba: ſa hoſt.
Finally, if the ſubſtantiue beginneth

La difference de, je, moy, tu, et, toy.

Cès quatre pronoms different ainſi :
je, eſt touſ⁓jours avec le verbe :
et, moy, eſt abſolu : commet : ſi je dy

{ qui ha fait cela ?

vous reſpondez, moy :
et non pas, je : ſi d'adventure vous ne re-
pétez toute la clauſe, ce qui eſt tédieus : comme

{ je l'ay fait.

Tu, et, toy, ſont de meſme : comme,

{ qui rit ? c'eſt toy, et non pas, tu.

D'aucuns pronoms poſſeſſifs.

MOn, ma, ton, ta, ſon, ſa, ſont de
meſme eſtofe que, bel, et beau :
pour éviter le baallement qui
s'enſuivroit, nous diſons :

{ mon ame, ton harbaleſte :

{ ſon hoſteſſe :

au lieu de, ma ame : ta harba : ſa hoſt.
Finalement, ſi le ſubſtantif ſe commence

Mon, ton,
ſon, ioyned
with words
beginning
by vowels.
Ma, ta, ſa,
with words
beginning
with conſo-
nants.

by a vowell, although it be of
the feminine gender, we ioyne vnto it
theſe maſculines, mon, ton, ſon.

Me, te, ſe, le, vous.

T*Heſe ſyllables are commonly ſet*
before verbes: as

{ je vouȿ prie: je te recommande:
I pray you: I recommend vnto thee:
il me bat: je le voy: il ſe courrouſſe:
he beateth me: I ſee him: he chafeth:
il ſe mocque: je me ry de toy:
he mocketh: I laugh at thee:

but if the queſtion be asked, then
vous, *and,* tu, *follow the verbe: as*

{ que diteȿ vous?
what ſay you?
que faiȿ tu?
what doeſt thou?

Nous, and, vous.

VV*Hen you find two,* vous, *together,*
take the one for the nominatiue caſe,
and the other for the accuſatiue, as

{ vouȿ vouȿ trompez:
you deceiue your ſelfe:
vouȿ tuereȿ vous?
will you kill your ſelfe?

nous, *is the like, as*

par vne voyelle, encor qu'il foit du
feminin, nous luy affocions
cès mafculins, mon, ton, fon.

Me, te, fe, le, vous.

Cès fyllabes font communément mifes
devant lès verbes, comme
je vous prie: je te recommande:

il me bat: je le voy: il fe courrouffe:

il fe mocque: je me ry de toy:

mais fi la queftion eft demandée, lors
vous, et, tu, fuivent le verbe, comme
que dites vous?

que fais tu?

Nous & vous.

QUand vous trouvez deux, vous, en-
femble, prenez l'un pour le nominatif,
et l'autre pour l'accufatif, comme
vous vous trompez:

vous tuerez vous?

nous, eft femblable: comme

nouſ nouſ lavons:
we waſh our ſelues:
nouſ ne nouſ mocquonſ pas.
we do not mocke.

Noz, and, voz.

*I*F *theſe words be ſet before*
ſubſtantiues, we ſay,
noʒ biens: voz amis:
our goods: your friends:
but after, ſay,
lèſ bois font noſtres eṭ voſtres:
the woods be ours and yours:
and the one before, and the
other after, ſay,
ce fonṭ noz amis, eṭ lèſ voſtres.
they be our friends, and yours.

En, le, la, and, y, relatiues.

E N, *rehearſeth the thing before ſpoken:*
as alſo, le, *and,* la: *as*
preſteʒ moy de l'argent:
lend me ſome money:
vous en aurez: où eſt mon père?
you ſhall haue of it: where is my father?
ne le voyeʒ vouſ pas?
do you not ſee him?
je ne le voy pas: où eſt la
J ſee him not: where is the
chambriére? appelez-la:
maiden?   call her:

nouʂ nouʂ lavons :

nouʂ ne nouʂ mocquonʂ pas.

Noz, et, voz.

SI cèʂ deuᶍ moţs fonţ miʂ devanţ fubftantifs, nouʂ difons,

noᵶ biens : voz amis :

mais après, dites,

lèʂ bois fonţ noftres, eţ voftres :

eţ l'un devant, eţ l'autre
après, dites,

ce fonţ noz amis, eţ lèʂ voftres.

En, le, la, et, y, relatifs.

EN, repéte la chofe devanţ dite :
commᵉ auffi, le, eţ, la, comme

preftez moy de l'argent :

vous en aurez : où eft mon père ?

ne le voyez vouʂ pas ?

je ne le voy pas : où eft la

chambriére ? appelez-la :

en, *ſometime is a prepoſition: as*

{ il eſt en la maiſon: en l'égliſe:
   he is at home,   *at church:*

en, *is ſometime put with verbes ſignifying*
mouing to a place, as

{ je vay en France:
   I go to France:
   vous en allez vous?
   go you your way?

y, *is an aduerbe rehearſing the place*
ſpoken before, as

{ Jehan eſt-il en la maiſon?
   is Iohn at home?
   ouy, il y eſt: allez à
   yea, he is therein: go to
   l'eſchole: j'y vay.
   ſchoole: I go thither.

Leur.

THis *word,* leur, *ſometime is a pronoune*
     poſſeſſiue: as

{ c'eſt leur droit:
   it is their right:

and *ſometime a relatiue of a thing*
ſpoken before: as eſt-ce le leur?
or, eſt-ce la leur? *for the feminine:*
ouy, c'eſt la leur.

aucune‿fois, en, eſt une prépoſicion, comme

{ il eſt en la maiſon: en l'égliſe:

en, eſt aucune-fois mis avec verbes ſigni-
fiants mouvement en quelque lieu, comme

{ je vay en France:

vous en allez vous?

y, eſt un adverbe repétant la place
devans mencionnée: comme

Jeḥan eſt-il en la maiſon?

ouy, il y eſt: allez à

l'eſcḥole: j'y vay.

Leur.

CE mot, leur, aucune‿fois eſt un pro-
nom poſſeſſif: comme

{ c'eſt leur droit:

et aucune‿fois un relatif de la choſe
devant dite: comme, eſt-ce le leur?
ou, eſt-ce la leur? pour le feminin:
ouy, c'eſt la leur.

Of the fubftantiue.

WE *follow the order of nature, putting*
the fubftantiue before the adiectiue: as

du pain blanc, de la biére de Mars, &c.
bread white,   beere of March:
but, bon, mauvais, bel, belle, petit,
    good, euill,   faire,   little,
and certaine others, be commonly
put before the fubftantiue: as

un bon home: une mauvaife fame.
a good man,   an euill woman.

Ne.

WHen *we denie, we vfe*
euer this fyllable, ne, *for*
a figne of denying, and it is moft often
accompanied with, point, pas, rien, nul,
perfonne, aucun, fauroy, oncques,
or, iamais: *as*

je ne veux point de cela: il ne fait pas
I will none of that: he doth not
ce qu'il ha dit: je ne voy perfonne:
that he hath faid: I fee no body:
je ne dy rien: il n'y ha aucune danger:
I fay nothing: there is no danger:
ne le veiftes vous iamais?
did you neuer fee him?
je ne le vei oncques.
I neuer faw him.

Du ſubſtantif.

NOus enſuyvonş l'ordre de nature, met-
tanţ le ſubſtantif devanţ l'adjeſtif: cõme
du paịn blanc: de la biére de Mars, &c.

mais, bon, mauvais, bel, belle, petit,

eţ quelques autres ſonţ communémenţ
miş devanţ le ſubſtantif, comme

un bon hoome: une mauvaiſe fame.

Ne.

QUanḍ nouş denions, nous uſonş
touſ-jourş de ceſte ſyllabe, ne, pour
ſigne de negacion, eſtanţ le plus ſouvent
accompagnée de, point, pas, rien, nul,
perſonne, aucun, ſauroy, oncques,
ou, jamais: comme

je ne veuх poinţ de cela: il ne faiţ pas

ce qu'il ḥa dit: je ne voy perſonne:

je ne dy rien: il n'y ḥa aucun danger:

ne le veịſteş vouş jamais?

je ne le veịi oncques.

VVhere you ſhall note, that the verbe
is alwaies placed betwixt, ne, and, point,
or ſuch like: as

⎰ je ne parle pas, &c.
⎱ *I do not ſpeake, &c.*

Degrees of compariſon.

PLus, *is the ſigne of the comparatiue,*
and tres, *of the ſuperlatiue: as*

⎰ grand, pluſ⌣grand, treſ⌣grand, &c.
⎱ *big,   bigger,   the biggeſt of all.*

bon, *hath his owne comparatiue, as*

⎛ bon, meilleur, treſ⌣bon: mauvais,
⎜ *good, better,   beſt of all: euill,*
⎜ pire, &c. petit, moindre, &c.
⎝ *worſe,   little, leſſer:*

bien⌣fait, mieux⌣fait, treſ⌣bien⌣fait.

Trees and fruites.

NAmes *of trees be of the maſculine*
gender: as

⎛ un pomier, le poirier:
⎜ *an apple tree, the peare tree:*
⎜ ſay, une ſaulx:
⎝ *a willow tree:*

but all the fruites be of the fem. gender: as

⎰ une ceriſe, la pome, &c.
⎱ *a cherrie,   the apple.*

Où vouſ noterez, que le verbe
eſt touſ⌣jourſ placé entre, ne, et, point,
ou ſemblables: comme

{ je ne parle pas, &c.

Degrez de comparaiſon.

PLus, eſt le ſigne du comparatif,
et, tres, du ſuperlatif: comme

{ grand, pluſ⌣grand, treſ⌣grand, &c.

bon, ha ſon propre comparatif, comme

{ bon, meilleur, treſ⌣bon: mauvais,

pire, &c. petit, moindre, &c.

bien⌣fait, mieulz⌣fait, treſ⌣bien⌣fait.

Arbres et fruicts.

NOmſ d'arbres ſont du genre
maſculin: comme

{ un pomier, le poirier:

dites, une faulx:

maiſ touſ lèſ fruicts ſont du genre fem. cōme

{ une ceriſe, la pome.

Nownes heteroclites.

W E *make the plurall number by adding,* s, *into the singular: as*

{ la fame, lèş fames: maifon, maifons:
the woman, women: a houfe, houfes, &c.

but thefe follow not the rule:

{ œil, yeuļx, genoil, genouļx, cheval,
an eye, eyes, knee, knees, horfe,
chevauļx, porc, pourceauļx.
horfes, hog, hogs.

Rules for Verbes.

T He *firft perfon fingular of the prefent tenfe of the indicatiue moode, ought to end in,* y, *meaning of thofe verbes which may leaue,* s: *as*

{ je fuy, je voy, j'oy je croy, j'eʃcry:
I am, I fee, I heare, I beleeue, I write:

and not, je fuis; *and this is not onely for the difference of the fecond perfon fingular of the fame tenfe and moode, but alfo to the likeneffe of all other firft perfons of the fingular number of all tenfes and moodes, which admit no,* s: *as*

{ j'aloy, j'alay, j'iray:
I did go, I went, I will go.

and not, j'alois: *excepting the Poets: but Verbes ending in,* rs, *and* ts,

Noms hétéroclites.

NOus faisons le nombre plurier en adjoustant, s, au singulier : comme

{ la fame, lès fames : maison, maisons :

mais ceux-cy ne suivent pas la reigle :

{ œil, yeulx, genoil, genoulx, cheval,

chevaulx, porc, pourceaulx.

Reigles pour les verbes.

LA premiére personne sing. du temps present de l'indicatif mœuf, se doibt terminer en, y, j'entend dès verbes qui peuvent laisser, s, comme

{ je suy, je voy, j'oy, je croy, j'escry :

et non pas, je suis : et cecy non seulement pour la difference de la seconde personne singuliére du mesme temps et mœuf, mais aussi à la similitude de toutes lès autres premiéres personnes du nombre sing. de tons lès temps et mœufs, lesquelz n'admettent point, s, comme

{ j'aloy, j'alay, j'iray :

et non pas, j'aloys : lès Poëtes exceptez : mais lès Verbes finissants en, rs, et, ts :

cannot ſpare, s, *for the quantities ſake,*
{ je pers, je meṭs.
{ *J leeſe, J lend.*

A ſhortning of verbes, called in Latin, Contraƈtio.

I*N ſtead of* je differeray, donneray,
je laiſſeray, demoureray, meneray,
we ſay,
{ je dorray, *or* donray, je lairray, je demorray,
{ *I will giue,   I will leaue, I will dwell,*
{ je marray,   differray,
{ *I will leade, deferre.*
    Likewiſe for c'eſt ḩome, ceſte fame,
à ceſte ḩeure, ceſt eſcu : *we ſay,* ſtome,
ſtefame, àſteure, ſtécu.

The future tenſe of the indicatiue.

T*He firſt perſon of this tenſe is commonly
formed of the firſt of the preſent tenſe
of the indicatiue, by adding,* ray, *as*
{ j'aime, j'aimeray : je ly,   je liray :
{ *I loue, I will loue : I reade, I ſhall reade :*
{ je prend, je prendray :
{ *I take,   I will take.*
Few be excepted :

ne peuvent laiffer, s, acaufe de la quantité,

{ je pers, je mets.

Abregement de verbes, appellé en Latin, Contraćtio.

AU lieu de, je differeray, donneray,
je laifferay, demoureray, meneray,
nous difons,

{ je dorray, ou donray : lairray : je demorray,

je marray, differray.

Semblablement au lieu de, ceft home, cefte fame, à cefte heure, ceft efcu : nous difons,
ftome, ftefame, àfteure, ftécu.

Le futur de l'indicatif.

LA premiére perfonne de ce temps, eft communément formée de la première du têps
prefent de l'indicatif, en y adjouftant, ray : côme

{ j'aime, j'aimeray : je ly, je liray :

je prend, je prendray.

Peu font exceptez.

je veulx, je vouldray :   je vay, j'iray :
I will,   I shall be willing: I go,   I will go:
je peulx, je pourray :   je fay, je feray :
I may,   I shall be able: I do,   I will do:
je fuy, je feray : j'ay,   j'auray :
I am,   I shall be: I haue, I shall haue:
je deçoy, je decevray :   je pers, perdray.
I deceiue,   I will deceiue: I lofe, I shall lofe.

je veulx, je vouldray : je vay, j'iray :

je peux, je pourray : je fay, je feray :

je fuy, je feray : j'ay, j'auray,

je deçoy, je decevray : je pers, perdray.

HARD WORDS

to breake the learner, and accuſtome
his tongue to the pronunciation of
the French.

E Saye, pluye, eſbahy, eſbahye, moyen, ouye, je l'ay ouye:
ayant, voyant, cotoyer, cotoyant: forvoyer, forvoyée, face,
grape, dame, l'ame, lame, courtoiſie, jalouſie, mauvaiſe, punais,
punaiſe, diſcorde, bouillonner, bouillon, fouiller, brouille,
brouillon, caille, caillé, taille, taillé, abiller, baillé, bailler,
grenoille, quenoille, magnanime, craignans, je gagne, gagner,
gagnans, cagnardier, rognon, mignon, yvrongner, Dieu, lieu,
milieu, ayeul, mieux, ieu, meur, peur, fuëur, je te louë,
bouë, faire la mouë, vaincu, vaincuë, un, une, d'un, d'une,
humble, aucun, chaſcun, quelcun, Ambrun, Autun, fus, ſoubz,
aragnée, une cognée, clouëe, entortillée, œil, deuil, cercueil,
ſueuil, orgueil, argenteuil.

AN ADVERTISEMENT
for Verbes Perſonals.

*A*LL *our verbes are declined after foure maner of waies: whoſe infinitiue endeth either in,* er, *as,* tomber, baller, aller: *in,* oir, *as,* vouloir, mouvoir, douloir: *in,* re, *as* faire, dire, lire: *in,* ir, *as* venir, trahir, envahir. *Now to the end that the Reader may with an eaſier way decline them, I haue ſet their ſeuerall examples, with faire and fit phraſes, in my Treatiſe of Verbes, printed and annexed to this worke, for that purpoſe, at the requeſt of diuers Gentlemen and Merchants: but namely at the commandement of that worthy Gentleman, to whom this worke is dedicated: knowing by experience what profit they gather by an vſuall declining as well verbes perſonals, as imperſonals.*

FINIS.

THE DATE OF THE FIRST EDITION
OF *THE FRENCH LITTELTON*

The first edition presents a bibliographical problem upon which it is unnecessary to dwell in detail as it has been fully dealt with by A. W. Pollard in 'Claudius Hollyband and his French Schoolemaister and French Littelton' (*Transactions of the Bibliographical Society*, vol. XIII (1916), pp. 253–72). The title-page is dated 1566, which is an impossible date for a book dedicated to Robert Sackville, 'sonne and heire to the honorable the Lord Burckhurst', when we know that Thomas Sackville did not become Lord Buckhurst until 8 June 1567, and that such evidence as there is points to the end of 1565 as the date of Holyband's arrival in this country. There are various other reasons, bibliographical and biographical, all equally cogent, which tell against 1566 and cannot be explained away. Moreover, acceptance of this early date for a book which in its dedication is described as a successor to *The French Schoolemaister* of 1573 would at once involve us in difficulties over this other date, and would mean that we should have to postulate the existence of an edition of the *Schoolemaister* in 1566 or earlier, of which no copy, nor trace of one, has ever been found. No one who takes the trouble to follow Pollard's argument can doubt that the 1573 *Schoolemaister* must be the first edition of Holyband's first book, and that the 1566 *Littelton*, which is admittedly his second work on the same subject, must therefore probably be misdated for 1576.

THE DEDICATEES OF *THE FRENCH LITTELTON*

Greater interest attaches both to the original dedicatee and to the patron to whom the fourth edition was transferred than to Sir William Herbert of Swansea to whom the fifth was inscribed in 1597. The first, as we have seen, was Robert Sackville (1561–1609), second Earl of Dorset, son to a more renowned father, Thomas Sackville, Lord Buckhurst, first Earl of Dorset, and father of a more renowned son, Richard Sackville, the third Earl. Robert won contemporary praise as 'a man of singular learning...Greek and Latin being as familiar to him as his own natural tongue'; but if he is remembered today it is as the 'little Robert Sackvile' for whose sake Roger Ascham set forth his theories of teaching in *The Scholemaister*.

Edward Lord Zouche, eleventh Baron, the patron of the 1593 edition, was also a man of parts, interested in scholarship but perhaps better known as a gardening enthusiast and a friend of Gerard the herbalist. When in 1587 he went abroad, partly in order to live more cheaply, Holyband accompanied him on his travels, and he speaks of him as almost a father to him and as the supporter of his old age more than lord and master. Holyband describes their European wanderings as 'long, lointain, penible et dangereux'. Zouche remained abroad until 1593, but Holyband presumably returned earlier as he had seen his *Dictionarie* through the press and dedicated it to Zouche by April of that year. Zouche was a man of about thirty when he set out on his travels: he died in 1625.

Neither A. W. Pollard nor Miss Lambley identifies Sir William Herbert of Swansea, and the latter refers to him erroneously as 'Lord Herbert'. Miss Farrer suggests that he was probably the son of Sir George Herbert of Swansea and a cousin of William Herbert, first Earl of Pembroke of that name. The connexion with Swansea certainly implies descent from Sir Richard Herbert of Ewyas in Herefordshire by Margaret, only child and heir of Sir Matthew Cradock of Swansea. Sir Richard was the illegitimate son of William Herbert, first Earl of Pembroke of the first creation. Sir George of Swansea was the second son of Sir Richard: his elder brother, William, became first Earl of Pembroke of the second creation. Sir George married Elizabeth, daughter of Sir Thomas Berkeley by Elizabeth daughter of George Nevill, Lord Abergavenny; and their eldest son, Matthew Herbert Esquire of Swansea, married Mary, daughter of Sir Thomas Gamage, by whom he had six sons and five daughters, the eldest being Sir William Herbert of Swansea. He was therefore the grandson of Sir George (d. 1570), not his son; and the great-nephew, not cousin, of William Herbert, first Earl of the second creation (1501-70). He died without legitimate issue in 1610. Matthew's second son, Sir John, died in 1617, aged sixty-seven, so Sir William must have been born before 1550; and, if I am right in identifying him with Holyband's patron, was probably a man of about fifty when this edition of the *Littelton* was dedicated to him. The usual genealogical sources do not help to establish his descent, but it is clearly done by G. T. Clark's *Limbus Patrum Morganiae et Glamorganiae* (1886), and by J. M. Traherne's *Historical Notices of Sir Matthew Cradock Knt. Of Swansea in the reigns of Henry VII and Henry VIII* (Llandovery, 1840). There is nothing to show whether he is the 'Sir William Herbert of Wales' who was knighted by Elizabeth in 1576.

APPENDIX C

HOLYBAND'S OTHER WORKS

There is no full-dress bibliography of Holyband: reference
should be made to Miss Farrer, discounting what she has to
say about the date of the first edition of the *Littelton*. Miss
Lambley's list supplements Miss Farrer's but gives insufficient
bibliographical data to supersede it, and does not locate the
copies. Stengel lists eighteen of Miss Farrer's exemplars and
adds three items which she was unable to see (*Chronologisches
Verzeichnis französischer Grammatiken*, 1890). The *Short-
Title Catalogue* lists ten editions of the *Schoolemaister* from
1573 to 1636 and ten of the *Littelton* from 1576 to 1630.
Omitting non-linguistic books, the following is a brief account
of his other works published in London.

*The Pretie and wittie Historie of Arnalt and Lucenda:
With certen Rules and Dialogues set foorth for the learner of
th'Italian tong* (1575) is a first reader and conversation manual,
with rules for pronunciation.[1] *Campo di Fior, or else The
Flourie Field of Foure Languages* (1583), which has four
parallel texts, Italian, Latin, French and English, is simply
a collection of dialogues on the usual subjects, without any
accompanying grammar rules. Incidentally, by appropriating

---

[1] This poses a bibliographical problem. The book is dated 1575, but
in dealing with the pronunciation of *gl* and *gn* Holyband concludes, 'as
I have more at larg taught both in my boke de pronuntiatione linguae gallicae
and in mine abregment of the French tong'. There is no evidence to suggest
that *De pronuntiatione* was published before 1580: it was entered in the Stationers' Register in September 1579. For a possible solution see p. 219 n. 1.

for it, without acknowledgments, the first eleven dialogues of Vives, Holyband becomes his first English translator. *The Italian Schoole-maister* (1580) incorporates the dialogues of *Arnalt and Lucenda* and expands and elaborates its rules.

The Treasurie of the French tong (1580) was his first attempt at compiling a good dictionary, to augment the *Schoolemaister's* vocabulary. With this latter, plus the *Littelton's*, it ultimately furnished the greater part of the material for his final work, *A Dictionarie French and English* (1593). For this last he drew upon several English predecessors and upon recent French lexicography, especially Nicot's enlarged edition of Thierry's *Dictionnaire françois-latin augmenté outre les précédentes impressions...* (Paris, 1573). But as Miss Farrer clearly shows, he was no mere copyist, and, apart from other improvements, must enjoy the credit of adding something like a thousand words to Nicot. Of greater interest to English readers is the relationship between his *Dictionarie* and Randle Cotgrave's more famous one of 1611. Cotgrave improves upon Holyband, both in method and arrangement: he adds many words, and his definitions are often more exact and helpful. Nevertheless, the *Stationers' Register* entries for 1608 and 1610 (Arber, III, 381, 432) carefully describe this later work as '*A Dictionarie* in Ffrenche and Englishe Collected first by C. Holyband and sythenc Augmented or Altered by Randall Cotgrave'. Miss Farrer's comparison of representative items makes it plain that 'quand on a dit tous les mérites de Cotgrave (et il a fait une œuvre vraiment originale), on lui aurait su gré de mentionner le modeste prédécesseur, auquel il devait tant. Cotgrave s'est tu, mais les registres ont parlé: ils ont revendiqué les droits de Hollyband et la justice s'est faite'.

A Treatise for Declining of Verbes (1580) is adequately described by its title, but it should be noted that Holyband called it 'the second chiefest worke of the French tongue' and that it went through five editions, according to the *Short-Title Catalogue*, to which Miss Farrer and Miss Lambley each add one more—a total which makes one inclined to question the former's comment, 'C'est peu de chose'. A more obvious interest attaches to his *De Pronuntiatione Linguae Gallicae* (1580) which is his only work written 'for the learned in the Latin tongue'. He had apparently been at work on it since 1576, or possibly even earlier.[1] It was dedicated to Queen Elizabeth, with whom, as he tells us, he had had the honour of speech when she visited Lewisham. One of the main purposes of this treatise was to set forth his own theories more fully than was possible in the *Littelton* which was a school-book: it also gave him opportunity to comment on the work of contemporary grammarians, and to discuss, with examples,

[1] Cf. p. 217 n. 1. In this 1580 publication he tells us that he has spent ten whole years teaching the Latin and French tongues in London, which, if taken literally, ought to imply from 1570 to 1580. But we know from the Returns of Aliens that he was teaching in 1568 and had arrived in England about 1565: we also know from the *Schoolemaister* that he had a school in Lewisham in 1573, and from the title-page of *Arnalt and Lucenda* that he had moved to the school in Paul's Churchyard by 1575. In the 1573 *Schoolemaister* he tells us that the captain of his school pronounced an oration before the Queen when she was 'now of late' at Lewisham: in the 1580 *De Pronuntiatione* dedication to the Queen he describes how she spoke to him 'cum tu *nuper* Lewshamiae rusticareris'— that is, 'lately' or 'recently'. The 'ten years', together with the removal from Lewisham by 1575, the use of the word 'nuper' in the dedication, and the reference to *De Pronuntiatione* in the text of the 1575 *Arnalt and Lucenda* all go to suggest that he was working on his Latin treatise and had penned his dedication as early as 1575 although it was not actually published until five years later.

the relative merits of the old and the reformed spelling and of his own practical compromise. To appreciate the comprehensiveness of the great work on the French language which he planned in the early 1570's, the *Littelton*, the *Treasurie* and the treatises on verbs and pronunciation must be regarded as four complementary and component parts of a single study.

For EU product safety concerns, contact us at Calle de José Abascal, 56–1°,
28003 Madrid, Spain or eugpsr@cambridge.org.

www.ingramcontent.com/pod-product-compliance
Ingram Content Group UK Ltd.
Pitfield, Milton Keynes, MK11 3LW, UK
UKHW010730190625
459647UK00030B/192